GHOSTS AND GHASTLIES

ILLUSTRATED BY BILL PROSSER
Franklin Watts / New York / London
1976

GHOSTS AND GHASTLIES

SELECTED BY HELEN HOKE

Library of Congress Cataloging in Publication Data
Main entry under title:

Ghosts and ghastlies.

CONTENTS: Hoke, H. About this book.—Brennan, J. P. The calamander chest.—Bulwer-Lytton, E.
The haunted and the haunters. [etc.]

    1. Ghost stories. 2. Ghosts—Juvenile poetry.
[1. Ghost stories. 2. Ghosts—Poetry. 3. Short stories]
I. Hoke, Helen, 1903–   II. Prosser, Bill.
PZ5.G327G34   [Fic]   76–13036
ISBN 0–531–01210–7

Contents

About this book

_ _ _ _ _ _ _ _ _ _ _ _ _ _ _ _ _

How would you feel if one night a chest in your bedroom opened of its own accord and you saw a long white finger protruding from under its lid? Or if you went into an empty room and the door mysteriously closed behind you and couldn't be forced open again? Pretty scared, I'll guess!

But though you wouldn't want such things actually to happen to _you_, I'll bet you get a kind of spooky thrill reading about them happening to someone else. If you're anything like me, you enjoy nothing better than being tucked up warm and safe in bed with a good ghost book—spooked to the marrow, even with your hair standing on end—but knowing at the back of your mind that it couldn't possibly happen to _you_.

If this sounds like you, then you are just the person for whom I have gathered together this collection of ghostly horrors. Well—most of them are horrible, but have you ever considered that a ghost could be more frightened than the person who was haunted? It doesn't sound possible, does it? But you will find such a ghost in this book.

Helen Hoke

Acknowledgments

The selections in this book are used by permission and special arrangements with the proprietors of their respective copyrights, who are listed below. The editor's and publisher's thanks to all who made this collection possible.

The editor and publisher have made every effort to trace ownership of all material contained herein. It is their belief that the necessary permissions from publishers, authors, and authorized agents have been obtained in all cases. In the event of any questions arising as to the use of any material, the editor and publisher express regret for any error unconsciously made and will be pleased to make the necessary corrections in future editions of the book.

"The Calamander Chest", by Joseph Payne Brennan. Reprinted by permission of Arkham House, Sauk City, Wisconsin.

"The Haunted and the Haunters", by Edward Bulwer-Lytton, as abridged by the compilers, from *Ghosts*, Aidan and Nancy Chambers, published by Macmillan Education Ltd., 1969.

"A Local Haunting", by Charles Causley, from *Underneath the Water*, published by Macmillan. Reprinted by permission of David Higham Associates, Ltd.

"The Haunted Mill", by Jerome K. Jerome, from *Told after Supper*. Reprinted by permission of The Society of Authors as the literary representative of the Estate of Jerome K. Jerome.

"The Fireplace", by Henry S. Whitehead. Reprinted by permission of Arkham House, Sauk City, Wisconsin.

"The Listeners", by Walter de la Mare. Reprinted by

The Calamander Chest

JOSEPH PAYNE BRENNAN

In which Ernest Maax buys an exotic chest of calamander wood for his lodgings, wondering why it had been sold to him so cheaply. . . . One evening, as he is sitting reading, his eye is drawn towards the chest. A long white finger protrudes from under the lid but, when he looks inside the chest, there is nothing there.

"FROM the Indies, sir!" said the second-hand dealer, pressing his palms together. "Genuine calamander wood—a rare good buy, sir!"

"Well—I'll take it," replied Ernest Maax somewhat hesitantly.

He had been strolling idly through the antique and second-hand shop when the chest caught his attention. It had a rich, exotic look which pleased him. In appearance the dark brown, black-striped wood resembled ebony. And the chest was quite capacious. It was at least two feet wide and five feet long, with a depth of nearly three feet. When Maax learned that the dealer was willing to dispose of it for only twelve dollars, he could not resist buying it.

What made him hesitate a little was the dealer's initial low price and quite obvious pleasure upon completing the transaction. Was that fine-grained wood only an inlay or did the chest contain some hidden defect?

9

When it was delivered to his room the next day, he could find nothing wrong with it. The calamander wood was solid and sound and the entire chest appeared to be in fine condition. The lid clicked smoothly into place when lowered, and the big iron key turned readily enough.

Feeling quite satisfied with himself, Maax carefully polished the dark wood and then slid the chest into an empty corner of his room. The next time he changed his lodgings, the chest would prove invaluable. Meanwhile it added just the right exotic touch to his rather drab chamber.

Several weeks passed, and although he still cast occasional admiring glances at his new possession, it gradually began to recede from his mind.

Then one evening his attention was returned to it in a very startling manner. He was sitting up, reading, late in the evening, when for some reason his eyes lifted from his book and he looked across the room toward the corner where he had placed the chest.

A long white finger protruded from under its lid.

He sat motionless, overwhelmed with sudden horror, his eyes riveted on this appalling object.

It just hung there unmoving, a long pale finger with a heavy knuckle bone and a black nail.

After his first shock, Maax felt a slow rage kindling within him. The finger had no right to be there; it was unreasonable—and idiotic. He resented it bitterly, much as he would have resented the sudden intrusion of an unsavoury roomer from down the hall. His peaceful, comfortable evening was ruined by this outrageous manifestation.

With an oath, he hurled his book straight at the finger.

It disappeared. At least he could no longer see it. Tilting his reading light so that its beams shot across the room, he strode to the chest and flung open the lid.

There was nothing inside.

Dropping the lid, he picked up his book and returned to the chair. Perhaps, he reflected, he had been reading too much lately. His eyes, in protest, might be playing tricks on him.

For some time longer he pretended to read, but at frequent intervals he lifted his eyes and looked across the room towards the calamander chest. The finger did not reappear and eventually he went to bed.

A week passed and he began to forget about the finger. He stayed out more during the evening, and read less, and by the end of a week he was quite convinced that he had been the victim of nothing more than an odd hallucination brought on by simple eye strain.

At length, at the beginning of the second week, deciding that his eyes had had a good rest, he bought some current magazines and made up his mind to spend the evening in his room.

Some time after he took up the first magazine, he glanced over at the chest and saw that all was as it should be. Settling comfortably in his chair, he became absorbed in the magazine and did not put it aside for over an hour. As he finally laid it down and prepared to pick up another, his eyes strayed in the direction of the chest—and there was the finger.

It hung there as before, motionless, with its thick knuckle and repulsive black nail.

Crowding down an impulse to rush across the room, Maax slowly reached over to a small table which stood near his chair and felt for a heavy metal ash tray. As his hand closed on the tray, his eyes never left the finger.

Rising very slowly, he began to inch across the room. He was certain that the ash tray, if wielded with force, would effectively crush anything less substantial than itself which it descended on. It was made of solid metal, and it possessed a sharp edge.

When he was a scant yard away from the chest, the finger disappeared. When he lifted the lid, the chest, as he had expected, was empty.

Feeling considerably shaken, he returned to his chair and sat down. Although the finger did not reappear, he could not drive its hideous image out of his mind. Before going to bed, he reluctantly decided that he would get rid of the chest.

He was in sound health and his eyes had had a week's rest. Therefore, he reasoned, whatever flaw in nature permitted the ugly manifestation rested not with him but with the chest itself.

Looking back, he recalled the second-hand dealer's eagerness to sell the chest at a ridiculously low price. The thing must already have had an evil reputation when the antique dealer acquired it. Knowing it, the unscrupulous merchant had readily consented to part with it for a small sum.

Maax, a practical young man, admitted the possibility of a non-physical explanation only with reluctance, but felt that he was not in a position to debate the matter. The preservation of stable nerves came first. All other considerations were secondary.

Accordingly, on the following day, before leaving for work, he arranged with his landlady to have the chest picked up and carted off to the city dump. He included specific directions that upon arrival it was to be burned.

When he arrived back at his room that evening, however, the first thing that met his gaze was the calamander chest. Furious, he hurried down the hall to his landlady's apartment and demanded an explanation. Why had his orders been ignored?

When she was able to get a word in, the patient woman explained that the chest actually had been picked up and carted off to the dump. Upon arrival, however, the man in charge of the dump had assured the men who lugged in the chest that there must be some mistake. Nobody in his right mind, he asserted, would destroy such a beautiful and expensive article. The men must have picked up the wrong one; surely there must be another left behind, he said, which was the worthless one the owner wanted discarded.

The two men who had taken the chest to the dump, not feeling secure in their own minds about the matter, and not wishing to make a costly mistake, had returned the chest later in the day.

Completely nonplussed by this information, Maax muttered an apology to the landlady and went back to his room, where he plopped into a chair and sat staring at the chest. He would, he finally decided, give it one more chance. If nothing further happened, he would keep it; otherwise he would take immediate and drastic measures to get rid of it once and for all.

Although he had planned to attend a concert that evening, it began to rain shortly after six o'clock and he resigned himself to an evening in his room.

Before starting to read, he locked the chest with the iron key and put the key in his pocket. It was absurd that he had not thought of doing so before. This would, he felt, be the decisive test.

While he read, he maintained a keen watch on the chest, but nothing happened until well after eleven, when he put aside his book for the evening. As he closed the book and started to rise, he looked at the chest—and there was the finger.

In appearance it was unchanged. Instead of hanging slack and motionless, however, it now seemed to be imbued with faint life. It quivered slightly and it appeared to be making weak attempts to scratch the side of the chest with its long black nail.

When he finally summoned up sufficient courage, Maax took

13

up the metal ash tray as before and crept across the room. This time he actually had the tray raised to strike before the finger vanished. It seemed to whisk back into the chest.

With a wildly thumping heart, Maax lifted the lid. Again the box was empty. But then he remembered the iron key in his pocket and a new thrill of horror coursed down his spine. The hideous digital apparition had unlocked the chest! Either that, or he was rapidly losing his sanity.

Completely unnerved, he locked the chest for a second time and then sat in a chair and watched it until two o'clock in the morning. At length, exhausted and deeply shaken, he sought his bed. Before putting out the light, he ascertained that the chest was still locked.

As soon as he fell asleep, he experienced a hideous nightmare. He dreamed that a persistent scratching sound woke him up, that he arose, lit a candle, and looked at the chest. The protruding finger showed just under the lid and this time it was galvanized with an excess of life. It twisted and turned, drummed with its thick knuckle, scratched frantically with its flat black nail. At length, as if it suddenly became aware of his presence, it became perfectly still—and then very deliberately beckoned for him to approach. Flooded with horror, he nevertheless found himself unable to disobey. Setting down the candle, he slowly crossed the room like an automaton. The monstrous beckoning finger drew him on like some infernal magnet which attracted human flesh instead of metal.

As he reached the chest, the finger darted inside and the lid immediately lifted. Overwhelmed with terror and yet utterly unable to stop himself, he stepped into the chest, sat down, drew his knees up to his chin and turned onto his side. A second later the lid slammed shut and he heard the iron key turn in the lock.

At this point in the nightmare he awoke with a ringing scream. He sat up in bed and felt the sweat of fear running down his face. In spite of the nightmare—or because of it—he dared not get up and switch on the light. Instead, he burrowed under the bedclothes and lay wide awake till morning.

After he had regained some measure of self-composure, he went out for black coffee and then, instead of reporting to his job, rode across town to the modest home of a truck driver and mover whom he had hired at various times in the past. After some quite detailed and specific plans had been agreed upon, he paid the mover ten dollars and departed with a promise to pay him an equal amount when the job was done. After lunch, considerably relieved, he went to work.

He entered his room that evening with a confident air, but as soon as he looked around, his heart sank. Contrary to instructions, the mover had not picked up the chest. It remained in the corner, just where it had been.

This time Maax was more depressed than angry. He sought out a telephone and called up the mover. The man was profusely apologetic. His truck had broken down, he explained, just as he was starting out to pick up the chest. The repairs were nearly completed, however, and he would absolutely be out to carry off the chest the first thing in the morning.

Since there was nothing else he could do, Maax thanked him and hung up. Finding himself unusually reluctant to return to his room, he ate a leisurely dinner at a nearby restaurant and later attended a movie. After the movie he stopped and had a hot chocolate. It was nearly midnight before he got back to his room.

In spite of his nightmare of the previous evening, he found himself looking forward to bed. He had lost almost an entire night's sleep and he was beginning to feel the strain.

16

After assuring himself that the calamander chest was securely locked, he slipped the iron key under his pillow and got into bed. In spite of his uneasiness he soon fell asleep.

Some hours later he awoke suddenly and sat up. His heart was pounding. For a moment he was not aware of what had awakened him—then he heard it. A furious scratching, tapping, thumping sound came from one corner of the room.

Trembling violently, he got out of bed, crossed the room and pressed the button on his reading lamp. Nothing happened. Either the electricity was shut off, or the light bulb had burned out.

He pulled open a drawer of the lamp stand and frantically searched for a candle. By the time he found one and applied a match to its wick the scratching sound had redoubled in intensity. The entire room seemed filled with it.

Shuddering, he lifted the candle and started across the room toward the calamander chest. As the wavering light of the candle flickered into the far corner, he saw the finger.

It protruded far out of the chest and it was writhing with furious life. It thrummed and twisted, dug at the chest with its horrible black nail, tapped and turned in an absolute frenzy of movement.

Suddenly, as he advanced, it became absolutely still. It hung down limp. Engulfed with terror, Maax was convinced that it had become aware of his approach and was now watching him.

When he was halfway across the room, the finger slowly lifted and deliberately beckoned to him. With a rush of renewed horror Maax remembered the ghastly events of his dream. Yet—as in the nightmare—he found himself utterly unable to disobey that diabolical summons. He went on like a man in a trance.

17

Early the next morning the mover and his assistant were let into Maax' room by the landlady. Maax had apparently already left for work, but there was no need of his presence since he had already given the mover detailed instructions in regard to the disposal of the chest.

The chest, locked but without a key, stood in one corner of the room. The melted wax remains of a candle, burned to the end of its wick, lay nearby.

The landlady shook her head. "A good way to burn the house down," she complained. "I'll have to speak to Mr. Maax. Not like him to be so careless."

The movers, burdened with the chest, paid no attention to her. The assistant growled as they started down the stairs. "Must be lined with lead. Never knew a chest so heavy before!"

"Heavy wood," his companion commented shortly, not wishing to waste his breath.

"Wonder why he's dumpin' such a good chest?" the assistant asked later as the truck approached an abandoned quarry near the edge of town.

The chief mover glanced at him slyly. "I guess I know," he said. "He bought it of Jason Kinkle. And Kinkle never told him the story on it. But he found out later, I figure—and that's why he's ditchin' it."

The assistant's interest picked up. "What's the story?" he asked.

They drove into the quarry grounds and got out of the truck.

"Kinkle bought it dirt cheap at an auction," the mover explained as they lifted out the chest. "Auction of old Henry Stubberton's furniture."

The assistant's eyes widened as they started up a steep slope with the chest. "You mean the Stubberton they found murdered in a . . ."

18

"In a chest!" the mover finished for him. *"This chest!"*

Neither spoke again until they set down the chest at the edge of a steep quarry shaft.

Glancing down at the deep water which filled the bottom of the shaft, the mover wiped the sweat from his face, "A pretty sight they say he was. All doubled up an turnin' black. Seems he wasn't dead when they shut him in, though. They say he must have tried to claw his way out! When they opened the chest, they found one of his fingers jammed up under the lid, near the lock! Tried to pick the lock with his fingernail, it looked like!"

The assistant shuddered. "Let's be rid of it, then. It's bad luck sure!"

The mover nodded. "Take hold and shove."

They strained together and in another second the calamander chest slipped over the edge of the quarry and hurtled toward the pool of black water far below. There was one terrific splash and then it sank from sight like a stone.

"That's good riddance and another tenner for me," the mover commented.

Oddly enough, however, he never collected the tenner, for that very day Mr. Ernest Maax dropped completely out of sight. He was never seen or heard of again. The disgruntled mover, never on the best of terms with the police, shrugged off the loss of the tenner and neglected to report the disposal of the chest. And since the landlady had never learned the mover's name, nor where he intended taking the chest, her sparse information was of no help in the search.

The police concluded that Maax had got into some scrape, changed his name, and effected a permanent change of locale.

The Haunted and the Haunters

EDWARD BULWER-LYTTON

In which a man and his servant spend a night in a haunted house. The first strange phenomenon is the footprint which suddenly forms itself before their eyes, followed by another—prints of a child's naked foot.

A FRIEND of mine, who is a man of letters and a philosopher, said to me one day, as if between jest and earnest, "Fancy! Since we last met, I have discovered a haunted house in the midst of London."

"Really haunted? And by what? Ghosts?"

"Well, I can't answer that question; all I know is this: six weeks ago my wife and I were in search of a furnished apartment. Passing a quiet street, we saw on the window of one of the houses a sign, "Apartments Furnished". The situation suited us; we entered the house, liked the rooms, engaged them by the week—and left them the third day. No power on earth could have reconciled my wife to stay longer; and I don't wonder at it."

"What did you see?"

"It was not so much what we saw or heard that drove us away, as it was terror which seized both of us whenever we passed by the door of a certain unfurnished room, in which we neither saw nor heard anything. Accordingly, on the fourth morning I told the woman who kept the house that the rooms did not quite suit us, and we would not stay out our week. She said, dryly, 'I know why: you have stayed longer than any other lodger. Few ever stayed a second night; none before you a third. But I take it they have been very kind to you.'

" 'They? Who?' I asked, affecting to smile.

" 'Why, they who haunt the house, whoever they are. I don't mind them; I remember them many years ago, when I lived in this house, not as a servant; but I know they will be the death of me some day. I don't care; I'm old, and must die soon anyhow. And then I shall be with them, and in this house still.' "

"You excite my curiosity," I said. "Nothing I should like better than to sleep in a haunted house. Pray give me the address of the one you left so ignominiously."

My friend gave me the address; and when we parted, I walked straight to the house. I found it shut up—no sign at the window, and no response to my knock. As I was turning away, a messenger boy said to me, "Do you want anyone at that house, sir?"

"Yes, I heard it was to be let."

"Let! Why, the woman who kept it is dead—has been dead these three weeks, and no one can be found to stay there, though Mr. Jones, the owner, offered ever so much. He offered Mother, who chars for him, £1 a week just to open and shut the windows, and she would not."

"Would not! And why?"

"The house is haunted: and the old woman who kept it was found dead in her bed, with her eyes wide open. They say the devil strangled her."

"Where does the owner of the house live?"

"In Jermyn Street, No. 11."

"What is he—in any business?"

"No, sir, nothing particular; a single gentleman."

I was lucky enough to find Mr. Jones at home. I told him my name and business. I said I heard the house was considered to be haunted; that I had a strong desire to examine it, and that I would be greatly obliged if he would allow me to hire it, though only for a night. I was willing to pay whatever he asked for that privilege.

"Sir," he said with great courtesy, "the house is at your service, for as short or as long a time as you please. Rent is out of the question. I cannot let it, for I cannot even get a servant to keep it in order or answer the door. Unluckily, the house is haunted, if I may use that expression, not only by night, but by day; though at night the disturbances are of a more unpleasant and sometimes of a more alarming character. The poor old woman who died in it three weeks ago was, in her childhood, known to some of my family and was the only person I could ever induce to remain in the house."

"How long is it since the house acquired this sinister character?" I asked.

"That I can scarcely tell you, but very many years since. The old woman I spoke of said it was haunted when she rented it between thirty and forty years ago. The fact is that my life has been spent in the East Indies, and I returned to England only last year."

"Have you never had a curiosity yourself to pass a night in that house?"

"Yes. I passed not a night, but three hours in broad daylight alone in that house. My curiosity is not satisfied, but it is quenched. I have no desire to renew the experiment. I honestly advise you not to spend a night in that house."

"My interest is exceedingly keen," said I, "and my nerves have been seasoned in such variety of danger that I have the

22

right to rely on them—even in a haunted house."

He said very little more. He took the keys of the house out of his bureau and gave them to me. Thanking him for his frankness, I carried off my prize.

Impatient for the experiment, as soon as I reached home I summoned my servant, a young man of gay spirits, fearless temper, and as free from superstitious prejudices as anyone I could think of.

"Francis," said I, "I have heard of a house in London which is decidedly haunted. I mean to sleep there tonight. From what I hear, there is no doubt that something will allow itself to be seen or heard—something, perhaps, excessively horrible. Do you think if I take you with me, I may rely on your presence of mind, whatever may happen?"

"You may trust me, sir!" answered Francis, grinning with delight.

"Very well. Here are the keys of the house; this is the address. Go there now, and select for me any bedroom you please. Since the house has not been inhabited for weeks, make up a good fire, air the bed well, and see, of course, that there are candles as well as fuel. Take with you my revolver and my dagger—so much for my weapons—and arm yourself equally well. If we are not a match for a dozen ghosts, we shall be a sorry couple of Englishmen."

I was engaged for the rest of the day on business. I dined alone, and about half-past nine I put a book into my pocket, and strolled leisurely towards the haunted house. I took with me a favourite dog—an exceedingly sharp, bold and vigilant bull-terrier; a dog fond of prowling about strange ghostly corners and passages at night in search of rats; a dog of dogs for a ghost.

It was a summer night, but chilly, the sky gloomy and overcast. Still, there was a moon—faint and sickly, but still a moon—and if the clouds permitted, after midnight it would be brighter.

I reached the house, knocked, and my servant opened with a cheerful smile.

"All right, sir, and very comfortable."

"Oh!" said I, rather disappointed; "have you not seen nor heard anything remarkable?"

"Well, sir, I must own I have heard something queer."

"What—what?"

"The sound of feet pattering behind me; and once or twice small noises like whispers close at my ear. Nothing more."

"You are not at all frightened?"

"I! Not a bit of it, sir," and his bold look reassured me that, happen what might, he would not desert me.

We were in the hall, the street door closed, and my attention was now drawn to my dog. He had at first run in eagerly enough, but had sneaked back to the door, and was scratching and whining to get out. After being patted on the head and gently encouraged, the dog seemed to reconcile himself to the situation and followed Francis and me through the house, but keeping close at my heels instead of hurrying inquisitively in advance, which was his normal habit in all strange places.

We first visited the kitchen and the cellars, in which there were two or three bottles of wine still left in a bin, covered with cobwebs and evidently undisturbed for many years. For the rest, we discovered nothing of interest. There was a gloomy little backyard with very high walls. The stones of this yard were very damp; and what with the damp and the dust and smoke-grime on the pavement, our feet left a slight impression where we walked.

And now appeared the first strange phenomenon witnessed by myself in this strange house. I saw, just before me, the print

24

of a foot suddenly form itself. I stopped, caught hold of my servant, and pointed to it. In advance of that footprint as suddenly dropped another. We both saw it. I went quickly to the place; the footprint kept advancing before me, a small footprint—the foot of a child. The impression was too faint to distinguish the shape, but it seemed to us both that it was the print of a naked foot. This phenomenon ceased when we arrived at the opposite wall, and it did not repeat itself as we returned.

We remounted the stairs, and entered the rooms on the ground floor, a dining parlour, a small back parlour, and a still smaller third room—all as still as death. We then visited the drawing-rooms, which seemed fresh and new. In the front room I seated myself in an armchair. Francis placed on the table the candlestick with which he had lighted us. I told him to shut the door. As he turned to do so, a chair opposite me moved from the wall quickly and noiselessly and dropped itself about a yard from my own chair, immediately in front of it.

My dog put back his head and howled.

Francis, coming back, had not observed the movement of the chair. He employed himself now in calming the dog. I continued to gaze at the chair, and fancied I saw on it a pale blue misty outline of a human figure, but an outline so indistinct that I could only distrust my own vision. The dog was now quiet.

"Put back that chair opposite me," I said to Francis. "Put it back to the wall."

Francis obeyed. "Was that you, sir?" said he, turning abruptly.

"I! What?"

"Why, something struck me. I felt it sharply on the shoulder—just here."

"No," said I. "But we have jugglers present, and though we

may not discover their tricks, we shall catch *them* before they frighten *us*."

We did not stay long in the drawing-rooms; in fact, they felt so damp and so chilly that I was glad to get to the fire upstairs. We locked the doors of the drawing-rooms—a precaution which we had taken with all the rooms we had searched below. The bedroom my servant had selected for me was the best on the floor: a large one, with two windows fronting the street. The four-poster bed, which took up much space, was opposite the fire, which burnt clear and bright. A door in the wall to the left, between the bed and the window, adjoined the room which my servant took for himself. This was a small room with a sofa-bed, and had no other door but the one leading into my bedroom. On either side of my fireplace was a cupboard, without locks, flush with the wall and covered with dull-brown paper. We examined these cupboards—only hooks to suspend dresses; nothing else. We sounded the walls—evidently solid: the outer walls of the building.

Having finished the survey of these rooms, I warmed myself a few moments and lighted my cigar. Then, still accompanied by Francis, went forth to complete my reconnoitre. In the landing-place there was another door; it was closed firmly.

"Sir," said my servant in surprise, "I unlocked this door with all the others when I first came; it cannot have got locked from the inside, for . . ."

Before he had finished his sentence, the door, which neither of us then was touching, opened quietly of itself. We looked at each other. The same thought seized both of us: some human agency might be detected here. I rushed in first, my servant following. A small blank dreary room without furniture . . . a few empty boxes and hampers in a corner . . . a small window, the shutters closed . . . not even a fireplace . . . no other door than that by which we had entered . . . no carpet on the floor, and the floor seemed very old, uneven, worm-eaten, mended here and there. But no living being, and no visible place in which a living being could have hidden. As we stood gazing round, the door by which we had entered closed as quietly as it had opened. We were imprisoned.

For the first time I felt a creep of undefinable horror. Not so my servant. "Why, they don't think to trap us, sir? I could break the door with a kick of my foot."

"Try first if it will open to your hand," said I, "while I unclose the shutters and see what is outside."

I unbarred the shutters; the window looked out on the little backyard I have described. There was no ledge—nothing to break the sheer descent of the wall. No man getting out of that window would have found any footing till he had fallen on the stones below.

Francis, meanwhile, was vainly attempting to open the door. He now turned round to me and asked my permission to use force. I willingly gave him the permission he required. But though he was a remarkably strong man, the door did not even shake to his stoutest kick. Breathless and panting, he stopped. I then tried the door myself, equally in vain. As I ceased from the effort, again that creep of horror came over me; but this time it was more cold and stubborn. I felt as if some strange and ghastly vapour were rising up from the chinks of that rugged floor.

The door now very slowly and quietly opened of its own accord. We rushed out on to the landing. We both saw a large pale light—as large as the human figure but shapeless and unsubstantial—move before us, and climb the stairs that led from the landing into the attics. I followed the light, and my servant followed me. It entered a small garret, of which the door

27

stood open. I entered in the same instant. The light then collapsed into a small globe, exceedingly brilliant and vivid; rested a moment on a bed in the corner, quivered, and vanished.

We approached the bed and examined it—a small one such as is commonly found in attics used by servants. On the chest of drawers that stood near it we saw an old faded silk scarf with the needle still left in a half-repaired tear. The scarf was covered with dust; probably it had belonged to the old woman who had last died in that house, and this might have been her bedroom. I had sufficient curiosity to open the drawers: there were a few odds and ends of female dress, and two letters tied round with a narrow ribbon of faded yellow. I took the letters.

We found nothing else in the room worth noticing, nor did the light reappear. But we distinctly heard, as we turned to go, a pattering footfall on the floor—just ahead of us. We went through the other attics (four, in all), the footfall still preceding us. Nothing to be seen—nothing but the footfall heard. I had the letters in my hand: just as I was descending the stairs I distinctly felt my wrist seized, and a faint, soft effort made to draw the letters from my clasp. I only held them the more tightly, and the effort ceased.

We returned to my room, and I then noticed that my dog had not followed us when we had left it. He was keeping close to the fire, and trembling. I was impatient to examine the letters; and while I read them, my servant opened a little box in which he had the weapons I had ordered him to bring. He took them out, placed them on a table close to my bed-head, and then occupied himself in soothing the dog, who, however, seemed to heed him very little.

The letters were short. They were dated, the dates exactly thirty-five years ago. They were evidently from a lover to his mistress, or a husband to some young wife. A reference to a voyage indicated the writer to have been a seafarer. The spelling and handwriting were those of a man poorly educated, but still the language itself was forceful. In the expressions of endearment there was a kind of rough wild love; but here and there were dark hints at some secret not of love—some secret that seemed of crime. "We ought to love each other," was one of the sentences I remember, "for how everyone else would curse us if all was known." Again: "Don't let anyone be in the same room with you at night—you talk in your sleep." And again: "What's done can't be undone; and I tell you there's nothing against us unless the dead could come to life." Here there was underlined in a better handwriting (a woman's), "They do!" At the end of the letter latest in date the same female hand had written these words: "Lost at sea the 4th of June, the same day as—."

I put down the letters, and began to think over their contents.

Fearing, however, that the train of thought might unsteady my nerves, I determined to keep my mind in a fit state to cope with whatever the night might bring. I roused myself, laid the letters on the table, stirred up the fire, which was still bright and cheering, and opened my book. I read quietly enough till about half-past eleven. I then threw myself, dressed, upon the bed and told my servant he might retire to his own room, but must keep himself awake. I bade him leave open the door between the two rooms.

Thus alone, I kept two candles burning on the table by my bed-head. I placed my watch beside the weapons, and calmly resumed reading. Opposite me the fire burned clear; and on the hearthrug, seemingly asleep, lay the dog. In about twenty minutes I felt an exceedingly cold air pass by my cheek, like a sudden draught. I fancied the door to my right, leading to the landing-place, must have got open. But no—it was closed. I then glanced to my left, and saw the flame of the candles violently swayed as by a wind. At the same moment the watch beside the revolver softly slid from the table—softly, softly—no visible hand—it was gone.

I sprang up, seizing the revolver with one hand, the dagger with the other. I was not willing that my weapons should share the fate of the watch. Thus armed, I looked round the floor. No sign of the watch. Three slow, loud, distinct knocks were now heard at the bed-head.

My servant called out, "Is that you, sir?"

"No. Be on your guard."

The dog now roused himself and sat on his haunches, his ears moving quickly backwards and forwards. He kept his eyes fixed on me with a strange look. Slowly he rose up, all his hair bristling, and stood perfectly rigid, and with the same wild stare. I had no time, however, to examine the dog. Presently, my servant came from his room, and if ever I saw horror in the human face, it was then. I would not have recognised him had we met in the street, so altered was every line.

He passed by me quickly, saying in a whisper that seemed scarcely to come from his lips, "Run—run! It is after me!"

He gained the door to the landing, pulled it open, and rushed out. I followed him into the landing, calling him to stop; but without heeding me, he bounded down the stairs, clinging to the bannisters, and taking several steps at a time. I heard the street door open—heard it again clap to. I was left alone in the haunted house.

For a brief moment I remained undecided whether or not to follow my servant. But pride and curiosity forbade a flight. I re-entered my room, closing the door after me, and went cautiously into my servant's room. I found nothing to justify his terror. I again carefully examined the walls to see if there

30

were any concealed door. I could find no trace of one—not even a seam in the dull brown paper with which the room was hung. How, then, had the THING, whatever it was, which had so scared him, got in except through my own chamber?

I returned to my room, shut and locked the door between the rooms, and stood on the hearth, expectant and prepared. I now saw that the dog had slunk into an angle of the wall and was pressing himself close against it, as if literally striving to force his way into it. I approached the animal and spoke to it; the poor brute was beside itself with terror. It showed all its teeth, the slaver dropping from its jaws, and would certainly have bitten me if I had touched it. It did not seem to recognise me.

Finding all efforts to soothe the animal in vain, and fearing that his bite might be as poisonous in that state as in the madness of rabies, I left it alone, placed my weapons on the table beside the fire, seated myself, and took up my book.

I soon became aware that something came between the page and the light—the page was overshadowed. I looked up, and I saw what I shall find it very difficult, perhaps impossible, to describe.

It was a Darkness shaping itself from the air in very undefined outline. I cannot say it was of a human form, and yet it was more like a human form, or rather shadow, than anything else. As it stood, wholly apart and distinct from the air and the light around it, its size seemed gigantic, the top nearly touching the ceiling.

While I gazed, a feeling of intense cold seized me. An iceberg before me could not have chilled me more. I feel convinced that it was not the cold caused by fear. As I continued to gaze, I thought—but this I cannot say exactly—that I distinguished two eyes looking down on me from the height. One moment I fancied that I saw them clearly, the next they seemed gone. But

31

still two rays of a pale blue light frequently shot through the darkness, as from the height on which I half believed, half doubted, that I had seen the eyes.

I strove to speak—my voice utterly failed me. I could only think to myself, "Is this fear? It is *not* fear!" I strove to rise—in vain; I felt as if I were weighed down by an irresistible force—that sense of utter inadequacy to cope with a force beyond man's, which one may feel in a storm at sea.

And now, as this impression grew on me, now came, at last, horror—horror to a degree that no words can convey. Still I retained pride, if not courage; and in my own mind I said, "This is horror, but it is not fear; unless I fear I cannot be harmed; my reason rejects this thing. It is an illusion. I do not fear."

With a violent effort I succeeded at last in stretching out my hand towards the weapon on the table. As I did so, on the arm and shoulder I received a strange shock, and my arm fell to my side powerless. And now, to add to my horror, the light began slowly to wane from the candles; they were not, as it were, extinguished, but their flame seemed very gradually withdrawn; it was the same with the fire—the light went from the fuel; in a few minutes the room was in utter darkness.

The dread that came over me, to be thus in the dark with that dark Thing, brought a reaction of nerve. I found voice, though the voice was a shriek. I remember that I broke forth with words like these: "I do not fear, my soul does not fear." And at the same time I found the strength to rise. Still in that profound gloom I rushed to one of the windows, tore aside the curtain, flung open the shutters. My first thought was—LIGHT. And when I saw the moon high, clear, and calm, I felt a joy that almost drowned the previous terror. There was the moon, there was also the light from the gas-lamps in the deserted street. I turned to look back into the room; the moon penetrated its shadow very palely—but still there was light. The dark Thing, whatever it might be, was gone—except that I could yet see a dim shadow, which seemed the shadow of that Thing, against the opposite wall.

My eye now rested on the table, and from under it there rose a hand, visible as far as the wrist. It was the hand of an aged person—lean, wrinkled, small—a woman's hand. That hand very softly closed on the two letters lying on the table: hand and letters both vanished. There then came the same three loud measured knocks I heard at the bed-head before.

As those sounds slowly ceased, I felt the whole room vibrate; and at the far end there rose, as from the floor, sparks or globes like bubbles of light, many-coloured—green, yellow, fire red, azure. Up and down, to and fro, hither, thither, as tiny will-o'-the-wisps the sparks moved slow or swift, each at his own desire. A chair was now moved from the wall without apparent aid, and placed at the opposite side of the table.

Suddenly, from the chair, there grew a shape—a woman's shape. It was distinct as a shape of life, ghastly as a shape of death. The face was young, with a strange mournful beauty: the throat and shoulders were bare, the rest of the form in a loose robe of cloudy white. It began sleeking its long yellow hair, which fell over its shoulders; its eyes were not turned towards me, but to the door; it seemed listening, watching, waiting. The shadow of the Thing in the background grew darker; and again I thought I beheld the eyes gleaming out from the top of the shadow—eyes fixed upon that shape.

As if from the door, though it did not open, there grew out another shape, equally distinct, equally ghastly—a man's shape, a young man's. It was in the dress of the last century. Just as the male shape approached the female, the dark shadow

33

started from the wall, all three for a moment wrapped in darkness. When the pale light returned, the two phantoms were in the grasp of the Thing that towered between them. And there was a bloodstain on the breast of the female. And the phantom male was leaning on its phantom sword, and blood seemed trickling fast from the ruffles, from the lace. And the darkness of the Shadow between swallowed them up. They were gone. And again the bubbles of light shot, and sailed, growing thicker and thicker and more wildly confused in their movements.

The cupboard door to the right of the fireplace now opened, and from it there came the form of an aged woman. In her hand she held letters, the very letters over which I had seen *the* Hand close; and behind her I heard a footstep. She turned round as if to listen, and then she opened the letters and seemed to read. And over her shoulder I saw a livid face, the face of a man long drowned—bloated, bleached, seaweed tangled in its dripping hair. And at her feet lay the form of a corpse, and beside the corpse there cowered a child, a miserable squalid child with famine in its cheeks and fear in its eyes. As I looked in the old woman's face, the wrinkles and lines vanished, and it became a face of youth—hard-eyed, stony, but still youth; and the Shadow darted forth, and darkened over these phantoms as it had darkened over the last.

Nothing now was left but the Shadow, and on that my eyes were intently fixed, till again eyes grew out of the Shadow—evil, serpent eyes. And the bubbles of light again rose and fell and mingled with the wan moonlight. And now from these globes themselves, as from the shell of an egg, monstrous things burst out. The air grew filled with them: larvae so bloodless and so hideous that I can in no way describe them except to remind the reader of the swarming life which the microscope brings before his eyes in a drop of water. Things

34

transparent, supple, agile, chasing each other, devouring each other. Forms like nothing ever seen by the naked eye.

The shapes came round me and round, thicker and faster and swifter, swarming over my head, crawling over my right arm, which was outstretched against the evil beings. Sometimes I felt myself touched, but not by them. Invisible hands touched me. Once I felt the clutch of cold soft fingers at my throat. I was still aware that if I gave way to fear I should be in bodily peril; and I concentrated all my faculties in the single focus of resisting, stubborn will. And I turned my sight from the Shadow—above all from those strange serpent eyes—eyes that had now become distinctly visible. For there, though in nothing else round me, I was aware that there was a WILL, a will of intense evil, which might crush down my own.

The pale atmosphere in the room now began to redden. The larvae grew lurid as things that live in fire. Again the room vibrated; again were heard the three measured knocks; and again all things were swallowed up in the darkness of the dark Thing, as if out of that darkness all had come, into that darkness all returned.

As the gloom retreated, the Shadow was wholly gone. Slowly as it had been withdrawn, the flame grew again into the candles on the table, again into the fuel in the grate. The whole room came once more into sight.

The two doors were still closed, the door leading to the servant's room still locked. In the corner into which he had pushed himself lay the dog. I called to him—no movement. I approached. The animal was dead. His eyes protruded, his tongue out of his mouth, the froth gathered round his jaws. I took him in my arms and brought him to the fire. I felt acute grief for the loss of my poor favourite. I imagined he had died of fright. But I found that his neck was actually broken. Had this

been done in the dark? Must it not have been by a hand as human as mine? Must there not have been a living person all the while in that room? I cannot tell. I cannot do more than state the fact.

Another surprising circumstance: my watch was restored to the table from which it had been so mysteriously withdrawn. But it had stopped at the very moment it was taken, and despite all the skill of the watchmaker, it has never gone since.

Nothing more happened for the rest of the night. Nor, indeed, had I long to wait before the dawn broke. Nor till it was broad daylight did I leave the haunted house. Before I did so, I revisited the little room in which my servant and I had been for a time imprisoned. I had a strong impression that from that room had originated the phenomena which had been experienced in my chamber. And though I entered it now in the clear day, with the sun peering through the filmy window, I still felt the creep of horror which I had first experienced there the night before. I could not, indeed, bear to stay more than half a minute within those walls.

I descended the stairs, and again I heard the footsteps before me; and when I opened the street door, I thought I could distinguish a very low laugh.

I went at once to Mr. Jones's house. I returned the keys to him, told him that my curiosity was gratified and related quickly what had passed.

"What on earth can I do with the house?" he said when I had finished.

"I will tell you what I would do. I am convinced from my own feelings that the small unfurnished room at right angles to the door of the bedroom which I occupied, forms a starting point for the influences which haunt the house. I strongly advise you to have the walls opened, the floor removed—indeed, the whole room pulled down."

Mr. Jones appeared to agree to my advice, and about ten days afterwards I received a letter from him saying that he had visited the house and had found the two letters I had described replaced in the drawer from which I had taken them. He had read them with misgivings like my own, and had made a cautious inquiry about the woman to whom they had been written.

It seemed that thirty-six years ago (a year before the date of the letters) she had married, against her family's wishes, an American of very suspicious character. In fact, he was generally believed to have been a pirate. She herself was the daughter of very respectable tradespeople, and had been a nursery governess before her marriage. She had a brother, a widower, who was considered wealthy and who had one child of about six years old. A month after the marriage, the body of this brother was found in the Thames, near London Bridge. There seemed some marks of violence about his throat, but they were not deemed sufficient to warrant any other verdict than that of "found drowned".

The American and his wife took charge of the little boy, the deceased brother having made his sister the guardian of his only child. And in the event of the child's death, the sister inherited. The child died about six months afterwards. It was supposed to have been neglected and ill-treated. The neighbours swore they heard it shriek at night. The surgeon who had examined it after death said that it was emaciated as if from lack of food, and the body was covered with bruises.

It seemed that one winter night the child had tried to escape...crept out into the backyard...tried to scale the wall...fell back exhausted, and had been found next morning on the stones, dying. But though there was some evidence of cruelty, there was none of murder. And the aunt and her husband had sought to excuse the cruelty by declaring the stubbornness and perversity of the child, who was said to be half-witted.

Be that as it may, at the orphan's death, his aunt inherited her brother's fortune. Before the first wedded year was out, the American left England suddenly, and never returned. He obtained a cruising vessel, which was lost in the Atlantic two years afterwards. The widow was left in wealth, but reverses of various kinds had befallen her and her money was lost. Then she entered service, sinking lower and lower, from housekeeper down to maid-of-all-work—never long retaining a place. And so she had dropped into the workhouse, from which Mr. Jones had taken her, to be placed in charge of the very house which she had rented as mistress in the first year of her wedded life.

Mr. Jones added that he had passed an hour alone in the unfurnished room which I had urged him to destroy, and that his impressions of dread while there were so great, though he had neither heard nor seen anything, that he was eager to have the walls bared and the floors removed as I had suggested. He had engaged men for the work, and would commence any day I named.

The date was fixed. We went into the dreary little room, took up the skirting boards, and then the floors. Under the rafters, covered with rubbish, we found a trap-door, quite large enough for a man to get through. It was closely nailed down with clamps and rivets of iron. On removing these, we descended into a room below, the existence of which had never been suspected. In this room, there had been a window and a flue, but they had been bricked over evidently for many years. With the help of candles we examined the place. There was some mouldering furniture, all in the fashion of about eighty years ago. In a chest of drawers against the wall we found, half rotted away, old-fashioned articles of a man's dress, such as might have been worn eighty or a hundred years ago by a gentleman of some rank—costly steel buckles and buttons, a handsome sword. In a waistcoat which had once been rich with gold-lace, but which was now blackened and foul with damp, we found five guineas, a few silver coins, and a ticket, probably for some place of entertainment long since passed away. But our main discovery was in a kind of iron safe fixed to the wall, the lock of which took much trouble to pick.

In this safe were three shelves and two small drawers. Ranged on the shelves were several small crystal bottles, sealed air-tight. They contained colourless liquids, which we discovered to be non-poisonous. There were also some very curious glass tubes and a small pointed rod of iron, with a large lump of rock-crystal and another of amber; also a magnet of great power.

In one of the drawers we found a miniature portrait set in gold, and retaining the freshness of its colours most remarkably, considering the length of time it had probably been there. The portrait was of a man who was perhaps forty-seven or forty-eight.

It was a remarkable face—a most impressive face. If you could imagine a serpent transformed into a man, you would have a better idea of that face than long descriptions can convey: the width and flatness—the tapering elegance and strength of the deadly jaw—the long, large, terrible eye, glittering and green as an emerald.

Mechanically, I turned round the miniature to examine the back of it, and on the back was engraved the date 1765. Examining still more minutely, I detected a spring; this, on being pressed, opened the back of the miniature as a lid. Inside the lid was engraved, "Marianna to thee—be faithful in life and in death to—." Here follows a name that I will not mention, but it was familiar to me. I had heard it spoken of by old men in my childhood as the name borne by a criminal who had made a great sensation in London for a year or so, and had fled the country on the charge of a double murder within his own house: that of his mistress and his rival.

We found no difficulty in opening the first drawer within the iron safe; we found great difficulty in opening the second: it was not locked, but it resisted all efforts, till we inserted the edge of a chisel. Inside, on a small thin book, was placed a crystal saucer: this saucer was filled with a clear liquid, on which floated a kind of compass with a needle shifting rapidly round. But instead of the usual points of a compass were seven strange characters, like those used by astrologers to denote the planets.

A peculiar, but not strong nor displeasing odour came from this drawer, which was lined with hazelwood. Whatever the cause of this odour, it affected the nerves. We all felt it, even the two workmen who were in the room—a creeping, tingling sensation from the tips of the fingers to the roots of the hair. Impatient to examine the book, I removed the saucer. As I did so the needle of the compass went round and round with great swiftness, and I felt a shock that ran through my whole body, so that I dropped the saucer on the floor. The liquid was spilt; the saucer was broken; the compass rolled to the end of the room. And at that moment the walls shook to and fro, as if a giant had swayed and rocked them.

The two workmen were so frightened that they ran up the ladder by which we had descended from the trap-door; but seeing that nothing more happened, they returned.

41

Meanwhile I had opened the book. It was bound in plain red leather, with a silver clasp. It contained but one sheet of thick vellum, and on that sheet were inscribed words in old monkish Latin, which literally translated were: "On all that it can reach within these walls—living or dead—as moves the needle, so work my will! Accursed be the house, and restless be the dwellers therein."

We found no more. Mr. Jones burnt the book and razed to the foundations the part of the building containing the secret room with the chamber over it. He had then the courage to inhabit the house himself, and a quieter, better-conditioned house could not be found in all London.

A Local Haunting

CHARLES CAUSLEY

Only one person knew her well:
The farmer's youngest, innocent son
Who, schoolwards, homewards, white as hail,
Would see her, break into a run,
To deaf ears tell his sweating tale.
There seems no doubt she gave him hell.

With the calm light her hands she'd lave,
Walking the clean, unprinted sand,
As from her shoulders fell a shawl
And the gaunt ring fell from her hand,
So the boy's tears each day would fall,
For he had seen her in her grave.

She crossed his vision like a snow
That he, and only he, could spy,
At noonday's heat, at morning's chill,
Wherever he might stand or lie
She kept her silent watch until
Light from the day began to flow.

43

Why she should choose him none could tell,
Or if she lay within his head.
At all events, he lost his grin,
Woke naked, screaming, in his bed,
Refused to speak, to eat, grew thin
While the frail shade grew strong and well.

Family, neighbours, turned aside.
Trembling, he thumbed his Bible page,
Hearing men speak of Bedlam, where
—Twice-locked within the human cage—
He knew he'd find her waiting there
To lie beside him like a bride.

At last, the rook-tailed priest, his wits
Propped with a rowan stick, a brass
Ring on his finger, creaking mouth
Of prayers, cut a raw star of grass,
Stood, as the custom, to the south,
Cautiously blew the ghost to bits.

What were the words she tried in vain
To speak to a child's unbruised heart?
The priest in his confessor's head
Kept her slow stain of speech apart,
And the boy's father, it was said,
Looked, somehow, more himself again.

And the sun rose, dispelled the vague
Irrelevant mist above the stream.
Softly the boy unclenched his fear.
His mother smiled, placid as cream:
In 1665, the year
Of the spruce, dog-eyed king, the Plague.

Yet all his life, with stiffening brow,
He waited for the ghost's return,
Paced the untenanted field. Afraid,
Alone, abstracted, he would burn
With love for the bitch of a shade,
Attend her voice, as I do now.

The Haunted Mill

JEROME K. JEROME

In which Joe Parkins takes a lease of an old mill which had been
occupied years before by a wicked old miser, who died leaving all his
money hidden there. Local gossips say that one day the ghost of the
miser will disclose the secret of the hiding-place.

WELL, you all know my brother-in-law, Mr. Parkins (began
Mr. Coombes, taking the long clay pipe from his mouth,
and putting it behind his ear: we did not know his brother-in-
law, but we said we did, so as to save time), and you know of
course that he once took a lease of an old mill in Surrey, and
went to live there.

Now you must know that, years ago, this very mill had been
occupied by a wicked old miser, who died there, leaving—so it
was rumoured—all his money hidden somewhere about the
place. Naturally enough, everyone who had since come to live at
the mill had tried to find the treasure; but none had ever
succeeded, and the local wiseacres said that nobody ever would,
unless the ghost of the miserly miller should, one day, take a
fancy to one of the tenants, and disclose to him the secret of the
hiding-place.

My brother-in-law did not attach much importance to the
story, regarding it as an old woman's tale, and, unlike his

predecessors, made no attempt whatever to discover the hidden gold.

"Unless business was very different then from what it is now," said my brother-in-law, "I don't see how a miller could very well have saved anything, however much of a miser he might have been: at all events, not enough to make it worth the trouble of looking for it."

Still, he could not altogether get rid of the idea of that treasure.

One night he went to bed. There was nothing very extraordinary about that, I admit. He often did go to bed of a night. What *was* remarkable, however, was that exactly as the clock of the village church chimed the last stroke of twelve, my brother-in-law woke up with a start, and felt himself quite unable to go to sleep again.

Joe (his Christian name was Joe) sat up in bed, and looked around.

At the foot of the bed something stood very still, wrapped in shadow.

It moved into the moonlight, and then my brother-in-law saw that it was the figure of a wizened little old man, in knee-breeches and a pig-tail.

In an instant the story of the hidden treasure and the old miser flashed across his mind.

"He's come to show me where it's hid," thought my brother-in-law; and he resolved that he would not spend all this money on himself, but would devote a small percentage of it towards doing good to others.

The apparition moved towards the door: my brother-in-law put on his trousers and followed it. The ghost went downstairs into the kitchen, glided over and stood in front of the hearth, sighed and disappeared.

Next morning, Joe had a couple of bricklayers in, and made them haul out the stove and pull down the chimney, while he stood behind with a potato-sack in which to put the gold.

They knocked down half the wall, and never found so much as a four-penny bit. My brother-in-law did not know what to think.

The next night the old man appeared again, and again led the way into the kitchen. This time, however, instead of going to the fireplace, it stood more in the middle of the room, and sighed there.

"Oh, I see what he means now," said my brother-in-law to himself; "it's under the floor. Why did the old idiot go and stand up against the stove, so as to make me think it was up the chimney?"

They spent the next day in taking up the kitchen floor; but the only thing they found was a three-pronged fork, and the handle of that was broken.

On the third night, the ghost reappeared, quite unabashed, and for a third time made for the kitchen. Arrived there, it looked up at the ceiling and vanished.

"Umph! he don't seem to have learned much sense where he's been to," muttered Joe, as he trotted back to bed; "I should have thought he might have done that at first."

Still, there seemed no doubt now where the treasure lay, and the first thing after breakfast they started pulling down the ceiling. They got every inch of the ceiling down, and they took up the boards of the room above.

They discovered about as much treasure as you would expect to find in an empty quart-pot.

On the fourth night, when the ghost appeared, as usual, my brother-in-law was so wild that he threw his boots at it; and the boots passed through the body, and broke a looking-glass.

49

On the fifth night, when Joe awoke, as he always did now at twelve, the ghost was standing in a dejected attitude, looking very miserable. There was an appealing look in its large sad eyes that quite touched my brother-in-law.

"After all," he thought, "perhaps the silly chap's doing his best. Maybe he has forgotten where he really did put it, and is trying to remember. I'll give him another chance."

The ghost appeared grateful and delighted at seeing Joe prepare to follow him, and led the way into the attic, pointed to the ceiling, and vanished.

"Well, he's hit it this time, I do hope," said my brother-in-law; and next day they set to work to take the roof off the place.

It took them three days to get the roof thoroughly off, and all they found was a bird's nest; after securing which they covered up the house with tarpaulins, to keep it dry.

You might have thought that would have cured the poor fellow of looking for treasure. But it didn't.

He said there must be something in it all, or the ghost would never keep on coming as it did; and that, having gone so far, he would go on to the end, and solve the mystery, cost what it might.

Night after night, he would get out of his bed and follow that spectral old fraud about the house. Each night, the old man would indicate a different place; and, on each following day, my brother-in-law would proceed to break up the mill at the point indicated, and look for the treasure. At the end of three weeks, there was not a room in the mill fit to live in. Every wall had been pulled down, every floor had been taken up, every ceiling had had a hole knocked in it. And then, as suddenly as they had begun, the ghost's visits ceased; and my brother-in-law was left in peace, to rebuild the place at his leisure.

"What induced the old image to play such a silly trick upon a

51

family man and a ratepayer?" Ah! that's just what I cannot tell you.

Some said that the ghost of the wicked old man had done it to punish my brother-in-law for not believing in him at first; while others held that the apparition was probably that of some deceased local plumber and glazier, who would naturally take an interest in seeing a house knocked about and spoilt. But nobody knew anything for certain.

The Fireplace

HENRY S. WHITEHEAD

In which a guest at the Planter's Hotel in Jackson, Mississippi, is visited by the ghost of a former occupant of the room, who has been dead for sixteen years. The ghost has a gruesome tale to tell of his demise at the hands of a party of poker players, and begs Mr. Callender's help in bringing them to justice.

But Mr. Callender is too busy with his own affairs for the next few years, and almost forgets his promise . . .

WHEN the Planter's Hotel in Jackson, Mississippi, burned to the ground in the notable fire of 1922, the loss to that section of the South could not be measured in terms of that ancient hostelry's former grandeur. The days had indeed long passed when a Virginia ham was therein stewed in no medium meaner than good white wine; and as the rambling old building was heavily insured, the owners suffered no great material loss. The real loss was the community's, in the deaths by fire of two of its prominent citizens, Lieutenant-Governor Frank Stacpoole and Mayor Cassius L. Turner. These gentlemen, just turning elderly, had been having a reunion in the hotel with two of their old associates, Judge Varney J. Baker of Memphis, Tennessee, and the Honourable Valdemar Peale, a prominent Georgian, from Atlanta. Thus, two other Southern cities had a share in the mourning, for Judge Baker and Mr. Peale both likewise perished in the flames. The fire took place just before Christmas on the twenty-third of December, and among the many sympathetic and regretful comments which ensued upon this holocaust was the many-times-repeated conjecture that these gentlemen had been keeping a kind of Christmas anniversary, a fact which added no little to the general feeling of regret and horror.

On the request of these prominent gentlemen, the hotel management had cleared out and furnished a second floor room with a great fireplace, a room long used only for storage, but for which, the late mayor and lieutenant-governor had assured them, the four old cronies cherished a certain sentiment. The fire, which gained headway despite the truly desperate efforts of the occupants of the room, had its origin in the fireplace, and it was believed that the four, who were literally burned to cinders, had been trapped. The fire had started, it appeared, about half an hour before midnight, when everybody else in the hotel had retired. No other occupant of the house suffered from its effects, beyond a few incidental injuries sustained in the hurried departure at dead of night from the blazing old firetrap.

Some ten years before this regrettable incident ended the long and honourable career of this one-time famous hostelry, a certain Mr. James Callender, breaking a wearisome journey north at Jackson, turned into the hospitable vestibule of the Planter's, with a sigh of relief. He had been shut up for nine hours in the mephitic atmosphere of a soft-coal train. He was tired, hungry, thirsty, and begrimed with soot.

Two grinning Negro porters deposited his ample luggage, toted from the railway station in the reasonable hope of a large emolument, promised by their patron's prosperous appearance and the imminence of the festival season of Christmas. They received their reward and left Mr. Callender in the act of signing the hotel register.

"Can you let me have number twenty-eight?" he required of the clerk. "That, I believe, is the room with the large fireplace, is it not? My friend, Mr. Tom Culbertson of Sweetbriar, recommended it to me in case I should be stopping here."

Number twenty-eight was fortunately vacant, and the new guest was shortly in occupation, a great fire, at his orders, roaring up the chimney, and he himself engaged in preparing for the luxury of a hot bath.

After a leisurely dinner of the sort for which the old hotel was famous, Mr. Callender first sauntered slowly through the lobby, enjoying the first fragrant whiffs of a good cigar. Then, seeing no familiar face which gave promise of a conversation, he ascended to his room, replenished the fire, and got himself ready for a solitary evening. Soon, in pyjamas, bathrobe, and comfortable slippers, he settled himself in a comfortable chair at just the right distance from the fire and began to read a new book which he had brought with him. His dinner had been a late one, and it was about half-past nine when he really settled to his book. It was Arthur Machen's *House of Souls*, and Mr. Callender soon found himself absorbed in the eerie ecstasy of reading for the first time a remarkable work which transcended all his previous second-hand experiences of the occult. It had, he found, anything but a soporific effect upon him. He was reading carefully, well into the book, with all his faculties alert, when he was interrupted by a knock on the door of his room.

Mr. Callender stopped reading, marked his place, and rose to open the door. He was wondering who should summon him at such an hour. He glanced at his watch on the bureau in passing and was surprised to note that it was eleven-twenty. He had been reading for nearly two hours, steadily. He opened the door, and was surprised to find no-one in the corridor. He stepped through the doorway and glanced right and then left. There were, he observed, turns in both directions at short distances from his door and Mr. Callender, whose mind was trained in the sifting of evidence, worked out an instantaneous explanation in his mind. The occupant of a double room (so he guessed) had returned late, and, mistaking the room, had knocked to apprise his fellow occupant of his return. Seeing at once that he had knocked prematurely, on the wrong door, the person had bolted around one of the corners to avoid an awkward explanation!

Mr. Callender, smiling at this whimsical idea of his, turned back into his room and shut the door behind him.

A gentleman was sitting in the place he had vacated. Mr. Callender stopped short and stared at this intruder. The man who had appropriated his comfortable chair was a few years older than himself, it appeared—say about thirty-five. He was tall, well-proportioned, and very well dressed, although there seemed to Mr. Callender's hasty scrutiny something indefinably odd about his clothes.

The two men looked at each other appraisingly for the space of a few seconds, in silence, and then abruptly Mr. Callender saw what was wrong with the other's appearance. He was dressed in the fashion of about fifteen years back, in the style of the late nineties. No one was wearing such a decisive-looking piccadilly collar, nor such a huge puff tie which concealed every vestige of the linen except the edges of the cuffs. These, on Mr. Callender's uninvited guest, were immaculate and round, and held in place by a pair of large, round, cut-cameo black buttons.

The strange gentleman, without rising, broke the silence in a well-modulated voice with a deprecatory wave of a very well kept hand.

"I owe you an apology, sir. I trust that you will accept what amends I can make. This room has for me a peculiar interest which you will understand if you will allow me to speak further, but for the present I confine myself to asking your pardon."

This speech was delivered in so frank and pleasing a fashion that Mr. Callender could take no offence at the intrusion of the speaker.

"You are quite welcome, sir, but perhaps you will be good enough to continue, as you suggest. I confess to being mightily puzzled as to the precise manner in which you came to be here. The only way of approach is through the door, and I'll take my oath no-one came through it. I heard a knock, went to the door, and there was no-one there."

"I imagine I would do well to begin at the beginning," said the stranger, gravely. "The facts are somewhat unusual as you will see when I have related them; otherwise I should hardly be here, at this time of night, and trespassing upon your good nature. That this is no mere prank, I beg that you will believe."

"Proceed, sir, by all means," returned Mr. Callender, his curiosity aroused, and keen. He drew up another chair and seated himself on the side of the fireplace opposite the stranger, who at once began his explanation.

"My name is Charles Bellinger, a fact which I will ask you kindly to note and keep well in mind. I come from Biloxi, down the Gulf, and, unlike yourself, I am a Southerner, a native of Mississippi. You see, sir, I know something about you, or at least who you are."

Mr. Callender inclined his head, and the stranger waved his hand again, this time as if to express acknowledgment of an introduction.

"I may as well add to this, since it explains several matters, though in itself sounding somewhat odd, that actually I am

57

dead."

Mr. Bellinger, at this astounding statement met Mr. Callender's facial expression of amazement with a smile clearly meant to be reassuring, and again, with a kind of unspoken eloquence, waved his expressive hand.

"Yes, sir, what I tell you is the plain truth. I passed out of this life in this room where we are sitting almost exactly sixteen years ago. My death occurred on the twenty-third of December. That will be precisely sixteen years ago the day after tomorrow. I came here tonight for the express purpose of telling you the facts, if you will bear with me and suspend your judgment as to my sanity. It was I who knocked at your door, and I passed through it, and, so to speak, through you, my dear sir!

"On the late afternoon of the day I have mentioned I arrived in this hotel in company with Mr. Frank Stacpoole, an acquaintance, who still lives in Jackson. I met him as I got off the train, and invited him to come here with me for dinner. Being a bachelor, he made no difficulty, and just after dinner we met in the lobby another man named Turner—Cassius L. Turner, also a Jacksonian—who proposed a game of cards and offered to secure two more gentlemen to complete the party. I invited him to bring them here to my room, and Stacpoole and I came up in advance to get things ready for an evening of poker.

"Shortly afterwards Mr. Turner and the two other gentlemen arrived. One of them was named Baker, the other was Mr. Valdemar Peale, of Atlanta, Georgia. You recognise his name, I perceive, as I had expected you would. Mr. Peale is now a very prominent man. He has gone far since that time. If you happened to be better acquainted here you would know that Stacpoole and Turner are also men of very considerable prominence. Baker who lives in Memphis, Tennessee, is

58

likewise a well-known man in his community and state.

"Peale, it appeared, was Stacpoole's brother-in-law, a fact which I had not previously known, and all four were well acquainted with each other. I was introduced to the two newcomers and we commenced to play poker.

"Somewhat to my embarrassment, since I was the host and the 'stranger' of the party, I won steadily from the very beginning. Mr. Peale was the heaviest loser, and although as the evening wore on he sat with compressed lips and made no comment, it was plain that he was taking his considerable losses rather hardly.

"Not long after eleven o'clock a most unfortunate incident took place. I had in no way suspected that I was not among gentlemen. I had begun, you see, by knowing only Stacpoole, and even with him my acquaintance was only casual.

"At the time I mention there began a round of jack-pots and the second of these I opened with a pair of kings and a pair of fours. Hoping to better my hand I discarded the fours, with the odd card, and drew to the pair of kings, hoping for a third. I was fortunate. I obtained not only the third king but with it a pair of eights. Thus, equipped with a full house, I considered my hand likely to be the best, and when, within two rounds of betting the rest had laid down their hands, the pot lay between Peale and me. Peale, I noticed, had also thrown down three cards, and every chance indicated that I had him beaten. I forced him to call me after a long series of raises back and forth; and when he laid down his hand he was holding four fours!

"You see? He had picked up my discard.

"Wishing to give Peale the benefit of any possible doubt, I declared the matter at once, for one does not lightly accuse a gentleman of cheating at cards, especially here in the South. It was possible, though far from likely, that there had been a

59

mistake. The dealer might for once have laid down his draw on the table, although he had consistently handed out the cards as we dealt in turn all the evening. To imply further that I regarded the matter as nothing worse than a mistake, I offered at once to allow the considerable pot, which I had really won, to lie over to the next hand.

"I had risen slightly out of my chair as I spoke, and before anyone could add a word, Peale leaned over the table and stabbed me with a bowie knife which I had not even seen him draw, so rapid was his action. He struck upwards, slantingly, and the blade, entering my body just below the ribs, cut my right lung nearly in two. I sank down limp across the table, and within a few seconds had coughed myself almost noiselessly to death.

"The actual moment of dissolution was painful to a degree. It was as if the permanent part of me, 'myself'—my soul, if you will—snapped abruptly away from that distorted thing which sprawled prone across the disordered table and which no longer moved.

"Dispassionately, then, the something which continued to be myself (though now, of course, dissociated from what had been my vehicle of expression, my body) looked on and apprehended all that followed.

"For a few moments there was utter silence. Then Turner, in a hoarse, constrained voice, whispered to Peale: 'You've done for yourself now, you unmentionable fool!'

"Peale sat in silence, the knife, which he had automatically withdrawn from the wound, still grasped in his hand, and what had been my life's blood slowly dripping from it and gradually congealing as it fell upon a disarranged pile of cards.

"Then, quite without warning, Baker took charge of the situation. He had kept very quiet and played a very conservative

61

game throughout the evening.

" 'This affair calls for careful handling,' he drawled, 'and if you will take my advice I think it can be made into a simple case of disappearance. Bellinger comes from Biloxi. He is not well known here.' Then, rising and gathering the attention of the others, he continued: 'I am going down to the hotel kitchen for a short time. While I am gone, keep the door shut, keep quiet, and clear up the room, leaving this (he indicated my body) where it lies. You, Stacpoole, arrange the furniture in the room as nearly as you can remember how it looked when you first came in. You, Turner, make up a big fire. You needn't begin that just yet,' he threw at Peale, who had begun nervously to cleanse the blade of his knife on a piece of newspaper; and with this cryptic remark he disappeared through the door and was gone.

"The others, who all appeared somewhat dazed, set about their appointed tasks silently. Peale, who seemed unable to leave the vicinity of the table, at which he kept throwing glances, straightened up the chairs, replaced them where they had been, and then gathering up the cards and other debris from the table, and threw these into the now blazing fire which Turner was rapidly feeding with fresh wood.

"Within a few minutes Baker returned as unobtrusively as he had left, and after carefully fastening the door and approaching the table, gathered the three others about him and produced from under his coat an awkward and hastily-wrapped package of newspaper. Unfastening this he produced three heavy kitchen knives.

"I saw that Turner went white as Baker's idea dawned upon his consciousness. I now understood what Baker had meant when he told Peale to defer the cleansing of his bowie knife! It was, as plans go, a very practical scheme which he had evolved. The body—the corpus delicti, as I believe you gentlemen of the law call it—was an extremely awkward fact. It was a fact which had to be accounted for, unless—well, Baker had clearly perceived that there must be no corpus delicti!

"He held a hurried, low-voiced conversation with the others, from the immediate effect of which all, even Peale, at first drew back. I need not detail it to you. You will have already apprehended what Baker had in mind. There was the roaring fire in the fireplace. That was his means of making certain that there would remain no corpus delicti in that room when the others left. Without such evidence, that is, the actual body of the murdered man, there could be as you are of course well aware, no prosecution, because there would be no proof that the murder had even been committed. I should simply have 'disappeared'. He had seen all that, and the opportunity which the fireplace afforded for carrying out his plan, all at once. But the fireplace, while large, was not large enough to accommodate the body of a man intact. Hence his hurried and stealthy visit to the hotel kitchen.

"The men looked up from their conference. Peale was trembling palpably. The sweat streamed from Turner's face. Stacpoole seemed unaffected, but I did not fail to observe that the hand which he reached out for one of the great meat knives shook violently, and that he was first to turn his head aside when Baker, himself pale and with set face, gingerly picked up from the table one of the stiffening hands. . . .

"Within an hour and a quarter (for the fireplace drew as well then as it does tonight) there was not a vestige left of the corpus delicti, except the teeth.

"Baker appeared to think of everything. When the fire had pretty well burned itself out, and consumed what had been placed within it piecemeal, he remade it, and within its heart placed such charred remnants of the bones as had not been

63

completely incinerated the first time. Eventually all the incriminating evidence had been consumed. It was as if I had never existed!

"My clothes, of course, had been burned. When the four, now haggard with their ordeal, had completed the burning process, another clearing-up and final re-arrangement of the room was undertaken. Various newspapers which they had been carrying in their coat pockets were used to cleanse the table. The knives, including Peale's, were washed and scrubbed the water poured out and the wash-basin thoroughly scoured. No blood had got upon the carpet.

"My not inconsiderable winnings, as well as the coin and currency which had been in my possession, were then cold-bloodedly divided among these four rascals, for such I had for some time now recognised them as being. There arose then the problem of the disposal of my other belongings. There was my watch, pocket-knife, and several old seals which had belonged to my grandfather and which I had been accustomed to wear on the end of the chain in the pocket opposite that in which I carried my watch. There were my studs, scarf-pin, cuff-buttons, two rings, and lastly, my teeth. These had been laid aside at the time when Baker had carefully raked the charred but indestructible teeth out of the embers of the first fire."

At this point in his narrative, Mr. Bellinger paused and passed one of his eloquent hands through the hair on top of his head in a reflective gesture. Mr. Callender observed what he had not before clearly noted, that his guest possessed a pair of extraordinary long, thin hands, very muscular, the hands of an artist and also of a man of determination and action. He particularly observed that the index fingers were almost if not quite as long as the middle fingers. The listener, who had been unable to make up his mind upon the question of the sanity of him who had presented this extraordinary narrative in so calm and convincing a fashion, viewed these hands indicative of so strong a character with the greatest interest. Mr. Bellinger resumed his narrative.

"There was some discussion about the disposal of all these things. The consensus was that they must be concealed, since they could not easily be destroyed. If I had been one of these men I should have insisted upon throwing them into the river at the earliest opportunity. They could have been carried out of the room by any one of the group with the greatest ease and with no chance of detection, since all together they took up very little room, but this simple plan seemed not to occur to them. Perhaps they had exhausted their ingenuity in the horrible task just finished and were over-anxious to depart. They decided only upon the necessity of disposal of these trinkets, and the actual disposition was haphazard. This was by a method which I need not describe because I think it desirable to show them to you."

Mr. Bellinger rose and led the way to a corner of the room, closely followed by the amazed Callender. Bellinger pointed to the precise corner.

"Although I am for the present materialised," he remarked, "you will probably understand that this whole proceeding is in the nature of a severe psychic strain upon me and my resources. It is quite out of the question for me to do certain things. Managing to knock at the door took it out of me, rather, but I wished to give you as much warning of my presence as I could. Will you kindly oblige me by lifting the carpet at this point?"

Mr. Callender worked his fingers nervously under the corner of the carpet and pulled. The tacks yielded after several hard pulls, and the corner of the carpet came up, revealing a large piece of heavy tin which had been tacked down over an ancient rat-hole.

"Pull up the tin, too, if you please," requested Mr. Bellinger. The tin presented a more difficult task than had the carpet, but Mr. Callender, now thoroughly intrigued, made short work of it, though at the expense of two broken blades of his pocket-knife. At Mr. Bellinger's further direction, inserting his hand, he found and drew out a packet of cloth, which proved on examination to have been fabricated out of a trousers pocket lining. The cloth was rotted and brittle, and Mr. Callender carried it carefully over to the table and laid it down, and, emptying it out between them, checked off the various articles which Mr. Bellinger had named. The round cuff-buttons came last, and as he held these in his hand, he looked at Mr. Bellinger's wrists. Mr. Bellinger smiled and pulled down his cuffs, holding out his hands in the process, and Mr. Callender again noted carefully their peculiarities, the long, muscular fingers being especially conspicuous, thus seen under the direct light of the electric lamp. The cuff-buttons, he noted were absolutely identical.

"Perhaps you will oblige me by putting the whole collection in your pocket," suggested Mr. Bellinger. Then, smiling, as Mr. Callender, not unnaturally, hesitated: "Take them, my dear man, take them freely. They're really mine to give, you know!"

Mr. Callender stepped over to the wardrobe where his clothes hung, and placed the packet in his coat pocket. When he returned to the vicinity of the fireplace, his guest had already resumed his seat.

"I trust," he said, "that despite the very singular—I may say, bizarre—character of my narrative and especially the statement with which I thought best to begin it, you will have given me your credence. It is uncommon to be confronted with the recital of such an experience as I have related to you, and it is not everybody who is—may I say privileged?—to carry on an extended conversation with a man who has been dead for sixteen years!

"My object may possibly have suggested itself to you. These men have escaped all consequences of their act. They are, as I think you will not deny, four thorough rascals. They are at large and even in positions of responsibility, trust and prominence in their several communities. You are a lawyer, a man held in high esteem for your professional skill and personal integrity. I ask you, then, will you undertake to bring these men to justice? You should be able to reproduce the salient points of my story. You have even proofs in the shape of the articles now in your coat pocket. There is the fact of my disappearance. That made a furore at the time, and has never been explained or cleared up. You have the evidence of the hotel register for my being here on that date and it would not be hard to prove that these men were in my company. But above all else, I would pin my faith for a conviction upon the mere recounting in the presence of these four, duly subpœnaed, of my story as I have told it to you. That would fasten their guilt upon them to the satisfaction of any judge and jury. They would be crying aloud for mercy and grovelling in abject superstitious fear long before you had finished the account of precisely what they had done. Or, three of them could be confronted with an alleged confession made by the other. Will you undertake to right this festering wrong, Mr. Callender, and give me peace? Your professional obligation to promote justice and set wrong right should conspire with your character to cause you to agree."

"I will do so, with all my heart," replied Mr. Callender, holding out his hand.

But before the other could take it, there came another knocking on the door of the hotel room. Slightly startled, Mr.

Callender went to the door and threw it open. One of the hotel servants reminded him that he had asked to be called, and that it was the hour specified. Mr. Callender thanked the man, and turning back into the room found himself alone.

He went to the fireplace and sat down. He looked fixedly at the smouldering fire in the grate. He went over to the wardrobe and felt in his coat pocket in search of negative evidence that he had been dreaming, but his hand encountered the bag which had been the lining of a trousers pocket. He drew it out and spread a second time that morning on the table the various articles which it contained.

After an early breakfast Mr. Callender asked for permission to examine the register for the year 1896. He found that Charles Bellinger of Biloxi had registered on the afternoon of the twenty-third of December and had been assigned room twenty-eight. He had no time for further inquiries, and, thanking the obliging clerk, he hastened to the railway station and resumed his journey north.

During the journey his mind refused to occupy itself with anything except his strange experience. He reached his destination in a state of profound preoccupation.

As soon as his professional engagements allowed him the leisure to do so, he began his inquiries by having looked up the owners of those names which were deeply imprinted in his memory. He was obliged to stop there because an unprecedented quantity of new legal business claimed his more immediate attention. He was aware that this particular period in his professional career was one vital to his future, and he slaved painstakingly at the affairs of his clients. His diligence was rewarded by a series of conspicuous legal successes, and his reputation became greatly enhanced. This heavy preoccupation could not fail to dull somewhat the sharp impression which the adventure in the hotel bedroom had made upon his mind, and the contents of the trousers pocket remained locked in his safe-deposit box undisturbed while he settled the affairs of the Rockland Oil Corporation and fought through the Appellate Division the conspicuous case of Burnet vs. De Castro, et al.

It was in the pursuit of a vital piece of evidence in this last-named case that his duties called him South again. Having obtained the evidence, he started home, and again found it expedient to break the long journey northward at Jackson. It was not, though, until he was actually signing the register that he noted that it was the twenty-third of December, the actual date with which Mr. Bellinger's singular narrative had been concerned.

He did not ask for any particular room this time. He felt a chill of vague apprehension, as if there awaited him an accounting for some laxity, a feeling which recalled the occasional lapses of his remote childhood. He smiled, but this whimsical idea was quickly replaced by a sombre apprehension which he could not shake off, and which emanated from the realisation that the clerk by some strange fatality had again assigned him room twenty-eight—the room with the fireplace. He thought of asking for another room, but could not think of any reasonable excuse. He sighed and felt a positive sinking at the heart when he saw the figures written down at the edge of the page; but he said nothing. If he shrank from this room's occupancy, this room with its frightful secret shared by him alone of this world's company with the four guilty men who were still at large because of his failure to keep his promise, he was human enough and modern enough in his ideas to shrink still more from the imputation of oddity which his refusal of the room on no sensible grounds would inevitably suggest.

He went up to his room, and, as it was a cold night outside, ordered the fire to be made up . . .

When the hotel servant rapped on his door in the morning there was no answer, and after several attempts to arouse the occupant the man reported his failure at the office. Later another attempt was made, and, this proving equally ineffectual, the door was forced with the assistance of a locksmith.

Mr. Callender's body was found lying with the head in the grate. He had been, it appeared, strangled, for the marks of a pair of hands were deeply imprinted on his throat. The fingers had sunk deeply into the bluish, discoloured flesh, and the coroner's jury noted the unusual circumstance when they sent out a description of the murderer confined to this peculiarity, that these marks indicated that the murderer (who was never discovered) possessed very long thin fingers, the index fingers being almost or quite as long as the middle fingers.

The Listeners

WALTER DE LA MARE

"Is there anybody there?" said the Traveller,
  Knocking on the moonlit door;
And his horse in the silence champed the grasses
  Of the forest's ferny floor:
And a bird flew up out of the turret,
  Above the Traveller's head:
And he smote upon the door again a second time;
  "Is there anybody there?" he said.
But no one descended to the Traveller;
  No head from the leaf-fringed sill
Leaned over and looked into his grey eyes,
  Where he stood perplexed and still.
But only a host of phantom listeners
  That dwelt in the lone house then
Stood listening in the quiet of the moonlight
  To that voice from the world of men:
Stood thronging the faint moonbeams on the dark stair,
  That goes down to the empty hall,
Hearkening in an air stirred and shaken
  By the lonely Traveller's call.
And he felt in his heart their strangeness,
  Their stillness answering his cry,
While his horse moved, cropping the dark turf,
  'Neath the starred and leafy sky;

71

For he suddenly smote on the door, even
    Louder, and lifted up his head:—
"Tell them I came, and no one answered,
    That I kept my word," he said.
Never the least stir made the listeners,
    Though every word he spake
Fell echoing through the shadowiness of the still house
    From the one man left awake:
Ay, they heard his foot upon the stirrup,
    And the sound of iron on stone,
And how the silence surged softly backward,
    When the plunging hoofs were gone.

Meeting With a Double

GEORGE D. PAINTER

When George began to climb all unawares,
He saw a horrible face at the top of the stairs.

The rats came tumbling down the planks,
Pushing past without a word of thanks.

The rats were thin, the stairs were tall,
But the face at the top was worst of all.

It wasn't the ghost of his father or mother,
When they are laid there's always another.

It wasn't the face of people he knew,
It was worse than this, shall I tell you who?

74

It was himself, oh, what a disgrace.
And soon they were standing face to face.

At first they pretended neither cared,
But when they met they stood and stared.

One started to smile and the other to frown,
And one moved up and the other moved down.

But which emerged and which one stays,
Nobody will know till the end of his days.

The Mistress in Black

ROSEMARY TIMPERLEY

In which a young teacher goes to a school to take up a new job as English mistress. But she is disturbed to find that no one else seems to be aware of the strange, silent young woman in black whom she is always meeting about the school...

THE school was deathly quiet and seemed to be deserted. Nervously I approached it from the road, followed a path round the side of the building and came to the main entrance. I tried the door but it was locked, so I rang the bell.

Footsteps approached. The door opened. A tall, pleasant-faced man with a grey moustache stood there.

"Good morning," I said. "I'm Miss Anderson. I have an appointment with the Headmistress at ten o'clock."

"Oh, yes. Come in, Miss. I'm the caretaker." He stood aside for me to pass and closed the door again. "If you'll wait here, I'll see if Miss Leonard is ready for you."

He went along the corridor in front of me, turned to the right and vanished.

With my back to the front door, I looked round the hall. On the wall to my left was a green baize notice-board with a few notices neatly arranged and secured with drawing-pins. I wondered whether that board would still be so tidy when the vacation was over and the children were back. Past the notice-board were swing doors opening on to an empty gymnasium, its equipment idle, its floor shining with polish. The paintwork was fresh and the place looked as if had just been redecorated. To my right were a number of other doors, closed and mysterious—for everything in an unfamiliar building seems mysterious. And ahead of me, to the left of the corridor and alongside it, was a flight of stairs leading upwards.

My nervousness increased. Interviews always panic me and I really needed this job. Trembling a little, I waited. The silence itself seemed to make a noise in my ears. I listened for the caretaker's returning footsteps.

Suddenly a woman appeared at the top of the stairs and began to descend. She startled me as she had made no sound in her approach, and I was reminded of one of my previous headmistresses whose habit of wearing soft-soled shoes had given her an uncanny ability to turn up silently when she was least expected. This woman on the stairs was pale, dark, very thin, and wearing a black dress unrelieved by any sort of ornament. Unsmiling, she looked at me with beautiful but very unhappy dark eyes.

"Miss Leonard?" I said.

She didn't reply or even pause, merely moved towards the doors of the gymnasium. At the same moment I heard the caretaker's returning footsteps and turned to see him re-enter the corridor.

"This way, dear," he called. "Miss Leonard will see you now."

As I went towards him, I thought I smelt something burning, so hesitated. Again I looked through the glass at the top half of the gymnasium doors. The woman in black was out of sight.

"What's the matter?" The caretaker came up to me. "Feeling nervous?"

"Yes, I am—but it's not that—I thought I smelt burning."

He looked at me sharply. "No, not now," he said. "That's

all over, and I should know. But I've got a bonfire going in the grounds. Maybe the smoke is blowing this way."

"That'll be it. Anyway, I can't smell it any more. Was that Miss Leonard I saw a second ago?"

"Where?" he asked.

"On the stairs, then she went into the gymnasium——"

"You're in a proper state of nerves, you are," he said, as I followed him along the corridor. "There's no one in the building today except you, me and Miss Leonard, and she's in her office waiting for you. Coming on the staff, are you?"

"I hope so. I've applied for the job of English teacher."

"Good luck, then," he said.

We stopped outside a door.

"This is Miss Leonard's room, Miss." He knocked on the door. A voice called: "Come in!"

And I went into the Headmistress's room.

Miss Leonard was at her desk, the window behind her. She rose immediately, a plump yet dignified figure with neat white hair and a pink suit which heightened the colour in her cheeks. She was utterly unlike the woman in black.

She smiled. "Do come right in and sit down, Miss Anderson. I'm glad to see you. It's not easy to find staff at a moment's notice at the end of the autumn term."

"It's not easy to find a job at this time either," I said. "Most schools are fixed up for the whole of the school year."

"We were too—then suddenly there was a vacancy. Now, you're twenty-five, you have a B.A. degree in English, and two years' teaching experience." She was looking at my letter of application which lay on her desk.

"That's right, Miss Leonard."

"You haven't been teaching for the past twelve months. May I ask why?"

"My mother and I went to live in Rome with my sister and her husband, who is Italian. Mother was ill and she wanted to see my sister again before—well, Mother's dead now so I decided to come back to England."

"And do you know anything about this school?"

"No. I simply answered your advertisement."

"I'm glad you did." She picked up a folder of papers and handed it to me. "In here I've enclosed your timetable for next term and details of syllabus and set books. So you can 'do your homework' before you arrive."

"You mean I've got the job?"

"Yes. Why not?"

"That's marvellous. Thank you."

We talked for a while then, as she took me back to the main door, she said: "You'll find the rest of the staff very nice and friendly."

"I think I've seen one of them already," I said.

"Really? Which one?"

"I don't know. It was just that she came down the stairs while I was waiting in the hall. She was wearing a black dress."

Miss Leonard said casually: "Staff do come back during the vacation sometimes, to collect forgotten property or whatever. Good-bye for the present, Miss Anderson. When you arrive on the first day of term, come to my office and I'll show you the staff room, then take you to your first class."

And the interview was over.

Christmas passed, January began, diligently I studied my folder of information and then, on the night before first day of term, snow fell. My lodgings were a train journey away from the school and on the very morning when I wanted to be punctual, my train stuck. Ice on the points. By the time I reached the school, I was late, and distraught.

Added to this, the school itself looked different under snow. I couldn't even find the path to the main door. I took a wrong path, lost myself wandering round the building, then peered through a classroom window.

Lights were on inside. About thirty-five little girls in white blouses and dark tunics were sitting at their desks and listening to the teacher. That teacher was the dark, thin woman in the black dress whom I had seen before. Fascinated, I stood and gazed. It was like watching a silent play, myself in the outside dark, the actors in the light, playing their parts.

In the front row of the class was a little girl with golden hair falling like bright rain over her shoulders. Next to her was a dark child, her black hair cropped close as a boy's. And next to this one was a child with a mop of red curls.

All the pupils were attentive, but this red-haired child was gazing at the teacher with an expression of adoration. It was touching, yet a little alarming. No human being deserves that much young worship. . . .

I retraced my steps along the wrong path in the snow, found the right one and finally reached the entrance door. It was not locked this time. I let myself in and hurried to Miss Leonard's room.

"Come in!" she called in answer to my knock.

As I went in I blurted out: "I'm so sorry I'm late. It was my train—the snow——"

"Never mind, Miss Anderson. I guessed as much. I'll take you to the staff room."

She led me up the stairs from the hall, along a first floor corridor, into a room. It was an ordinary staff room—notice-board, lockers, tables, hard chairs, easy chairs, electric fire. The light was on but the room was empty—at least, I thought it was empty at first, then realized that someone was sitting in one of the chairs. I saw her only out of the corner of my eye, and she was in a chair in the far corner of the room, away from the fire; so although I recognized her as the woman in black, I didn't turn to look at her. If I thought anything, it was just that she had a bit of a nerve to leave her class, which I'd seen her teaching a few minutes ago, and come to sit in the staff room—and now she's been caught out by the entrance of the Headmistress.

Miss Leonard, however, took no notice of her. She said: "This will be your locker, Miss Anderson. The bell will ring any minute now for the end of first period, then I'll take you to your first class. It's a double-period of English—you'll have seen that from your timetable. Mrs. Gage is looking after them at the moment—she's our biology teacher—and she'll be glad to see you as by rights these first two periods should be her free ones. That's why the staff room is empty."

But the staff room was not empty. There was the woman in black, looking at me seriously, with those beautiful sad dark eyes. . . .

Miss Leonard led the way to my first class. The teacher there looked quickly round as we entered. She was a lively, dark, fairly young woman with eagerly bent shoulders and black-rimmed spectacles. She wore a red sweater and brown skirt.

"Here we are, Mrs. Gage," said Miss Leonard. "Now you'll get your second free period all right." She faced the class. "Now, girls, this is Miss Anderson, your new English teacher. Help her as much as you can, won't you?"

And I too stood facing the class. It was the same class which I had seen through the window only fifteen minutes earlier. There was the child with fair hair in the front row, and the dark one next to her—and. . . .

No. It was different. The child with curly red hair was not there. Her desk was empty. And, of course, the teacher was different....

Miss Leonard and Mrs. Gage left the room. I was on my own with this familiar, unfamiliar class. I spent the next forty minutes or so in trying to get to know them, checking on their set books, and so on, then the bell rang for morning break and I returned to the staff room.

The chair where the woman in black had been sitting was empty now but other chairs were occupied. The staff had gathered for elevenses. I heard someone say, above the noise of the many voices: "How does that damned chair get over into the corner like that? Who puts it there?"

"Night cleaners have strange ways," said another voice.

"Extraordinary about night cleaners," said the first. "They work here for years, and so do we—and which of us are the ghosts? We co-exist, but never meet."

A woman in an overall came in with a tray bearing a pot of coffee and cups and saucers. Mrs. Gage came over to me. "Coffee, Miss Anderson?"

"Oh—thank you."

"How do you like it?"

"Black. No sugar."

"Same here." She collected coffee for us both.

"Sorry you missed a free period because of me," I said. "My train got held up in the snow."

"That's all right."

Sipping my coffee, I studied the other women around me.

"Doesn't everyone come here for coffee at break?" I asked Mrs. Gage.

"Everyone! It's only our elevenses that keep us going."

"Then where is—well—one of the teachers? She was taking

83

your class—my class—this morning—I saw her through the window—"

"Not that class," said Mrs. Gage. "I started with them immediately after morning assembly."

"But it *was* that class. I recognized some of the girls. And the one with red hair wasn't there."

Mrs. Gage looked at me sympathetically. "You're all upset over being late, aren't you? And maybe you're upset for other reasons too. I don't blame you. It's not easy to be taking Miss Carey's place."

"Miss Carey? Who——" But as I tried to ask more, the woman in the overall came to collect our dirty cups and the bell rang for third period. We all went off to our classes.

I still had one more period with the same class I'd taken before—or so I thought, until I reached the room. Then I saw that the teacher's chair was already occupied.

The woman in black sat there.

And the child with red hair was in the third desk in the front row.

"Sorry," I murmured, withdrew again, and stood in the corridor to re-examine my timetable. Surely I hadn't made a mistake—no—I was right—this was my class. So I went back. And the teacher's chair was empty now. So was the third desk in the front row. . . .

That was when I began to be afraid. So afraid that a sick shiver travelled down my spine, sweat sprang out on my skin, and I needed all my self-control to face the class and give a lesson.

At the end of the lesson, when the bell rang for next period, I asked the class in general: "Where's the girl who sits there?" I indicated the third desk in the front row.

No one answered. The children became unnaturally quiet

and stared at me.

"Well?" I said.

Then the fair-haired child said: "No one sits there, Miss." And the dark child next to her added: "That was Joan's desk."

"But where is Joan?"

Silence again.

Then Mrs. Gage walked in. "Hello, Miss Anderson. We seem to be playing Box and Cox this morning. Do you know which class to go to for last period?"

"Yes, thank you. I've got my timetable." I hurried away.

Busyness is the best panacea for fear, and I was very busy getting to know a different class until the bell rang for lunch. Back to the staff room again—and it was full again—and there was Mrs. Gage, kindly taking me under her wing.

"Miss Leonard asked me to look after you until you can find your way around," she said. "The staff dining-room is on the second floor. Would you like to come up with me?"

I was glad of the offer.

The staff, all female, sat at three long tables in the dining-room, and the place was as noisy as a classroom before the teacher arrives! Two overalled women, one of whom I had seen at break, served our meal. Conversation was mostly "shop"—the besetting sin of female teachers. As the newcomer, I kept quiet, but I looked at those women one by one, trying to identify the woman in black.

She wasn't there.

Unhungry, I did my best with the meat pie and carrots, then when rice pudding and prunes arrived (for teachers have children's diet) I murmured to Mrs. Gage: "Who is the member of staff who wears a black dress?"

She looked round. "No one, as far as I can see."

"No—she's not here—but I've seen her."

85

"Really? But I think everyone's here today. We do go out for lunch sometimes, but when the weather is like this it's easier to have it on the premises. What was she like?"

"Dark, pale, thin, not very young—with lovely eyes——"

"And wearing a black dress, you said?"

"Yes."

Mrs. Gage gave a small, unamused laugh. "Sounds like Miss Carey, but you can't possibly have seen her."

"The one who's left—whose place I've taken——"

"No-one could take Joanna's place."

"Oh—I didn't mean——"

"Miss Anderson, I'm sorry. I didn't mean anything either." She didn't look at me, but she had stopped eating her prunes.

"Did something bad happen to her?" I asked.

"She tried to burn down the school."

The words were whispered and the noise of voices around us was so loud that I thought I must have misheard, so I said: "What?"

"She tried to burn down the school," Mrs. Gage repeated. Others at our table heard her this time. Conversation faded, ceased. Heads turned towards Mrs. Gage.

"Don't all look at me like that," said Mrs. Gage. "I'm only telling Miss Anderson what happened last term. She has a right to know." Leaving her sweet unfinished, she pushed back her chair with a scraping noise and left the room. I sat petrified. Murmurs of conversation began again, but no one spoke to me, so I pretended to eat a little more, then rose and left.

I found my way back to the staff room.

Mrs. Gage, cigarette in hand, was sitting by the electric fire. "Sorry about that," she said. "Until you asked, I presumed you knew. It was in the newspapers."

"I've been living in Italy. I only came back just before

Christmas. Could you tell me what happened, before the others return from lunch?"

"Sure. Have a fag. Rotten first day for you." She passed me a cigarette and lit it for me.

"This smell of burning," I said. "I've noticed it before."

"It's only our cigarettes, Miss Anderson. And we'd better get them smoked before the rest of the staff come back. Some of them abhor cigarette smoke. These spinsters!"

"I'm one too."

"Not really. You're still young. So you want to know about Joanna Carey?"

"Of course I do. After all, I've seen her. Did she get the sack, and now she comes back uninvited—or what?"

"My dear child, you can't have seen her. She's dead."

"Then whom did I see?"

Mrs. Gage ignored this question. She said: "Miss Carey, Joanna, had been a teacher here for twenty years. She was excellent at her job and the kids adored her. Then, about a year ago, she changed."

"In what way?"

"Not in the way she taught. Her teaching was always brilliant. But in her attitude. After being most understanding and sympathetic with the young, she gradually became more and more cynical, to the point of cruelty. She made it clear to all of us, staff and pupils, that she now hated her job and only went on doing it because she had to earn a living somehow."

"But why did this happen?"

"Why? Who knows why anything? But in fact I do know more about her than most of the staff. Joanna and I were friends, before she changed. She often visited my husband and me, in the old days. She and I had occasional heart-to-hearts over the washing-up. So I learned something of her private life. She loved a married man, for about ten years. That *was* her private life. Then he ditched her—decided to 'be a good boy' again. When it happened, she told me, and she laughed, and didn't seem to care very much. But it was from that moment that she began to change, grow bitter, disillusioned. The world went stale for her. The salt had lost its savour. She began to take revenge, not against the man, but against everyone else with whom she came into contact. That meant us—staff and kids. She was filled with hate, and hate breeds hate. Even I, who had been her friend, began to avoid her. She was left alone."

"You said she tried to burn down the school."

"She did. She failed in that. But while she was trying, she burned herself to death. And one of the children."

"One of the children? Oh, no!"

"It's true, Miss Anderson. I wouldn't say it if it weren't. I, of all people, once so friendly with Joanna—I'd be the last person to admit it, if it weren't true. But it happened."

"What exactly did happen?"

"One Friday evening, towards the end of last term, she came back to school. This is what the police found out when they investigated afterwards. Everyone except Mr. Brown, the caretaker, had gone. She soaked the base of the long curtains in the gymnasium with paraffin and set fire to them. Imagine the flare-up that would make—all those curtains in that big room. Why she didn't get away afterwards, no one knows. Maybe she fainted. Maybe she deliberately *let* herself be burned—like that Czech student—you know. People do these things. When they're desperate. Mr. Brown saw the flames, sent for the fire service, and after they'd come and put out the fire, her body was found among the ashes of the curtains."

"And the child? You said—"

"Yes. Little Joan Hanley. A dear little girl with red curly hair. She adored Joanna. She was found there too, burned to death, among the ashes of the curtains."

"But how did she come to be there in the first place?"

"Once again, no-one knows. She was one of Joanna's worshippers. There were several in the school. Girls' schools are diabolical in this respect. Rather like all-female wards in hospitals. Joan Hanley would have done anything in the world for Joanna Carey. So did Joanna invite the child to the 'party'? I don't know. But it looks like it."

"Didn't the police find out anything about why Joan Hanley was there?"

"They tried. She had told her parents that she was going to the cinema, which she often did on Friday nights. When she didn't come home at her usual time, her parents wondered—and the next thing they knew, the police were on their doorstep, telling them that their daughter had been burned to death at the school. That's all I know, Miss Anderson—all any of us knows. Since it happened, workmen have put the gymnasium to rights, hence all the fresh paint and the pretty new curtains. These tragedies are happening all the time, all over the world—I know that—but when I think of Joanna, in her hatred and bitterness, drawing a child into such a burning—Oh, God!" She put her hands over her face.

The staff room became deathly quiet. Only the two of us there, Mrs. Gage and me, crouching over the electric fire, our cigarettes burning down, the silent snow covering the world outside—and God knows why I suddenly looked behind me.

I looked at that chair in the far corner of the room. It was no longer empty. The woman in black sat there. She looked straight at me, with those tragic eyes.

Then the staff room door burst open and the other women

89

poured in, filling the quietness with noise, filling the empty chairs with bodies, talking "shop"—and I thought: No wonder Joanna Carey took a hate against all this. And yet—to burn a child—along with oneself—No!

"I didn't!" The sound came over, clearly, loudly, as if it filled the world. Yet no one seemed to hear it. It had spoken into my head only.

"I'll prove it," said the loud voice in my head. "Come!"

Mrs. Gage was leaning back in the chair by the fire. She had lit another cigarette and closed her eyes. She looked tired out, and no wonder. I got up and left the room, that room full of talking women.

I walked, blindly, yet guided, along the unfamiliar corridors. Outside, in the snow, the children were having snowball battles. They were having a lovely lunch-hour! Heaven was outside. Hell was within.

I walked, without knowing why, into the classroom which I had seen through the window, the classroom where I had taught during the second and third periods of the school morning.

I walked up to the third desk in the front row.

I sat down at that desk, as if I were the little girl, Joan Hanley, who had, day after day, sat down at that desk. . . .

I opened the desk lid. There was nothing inside.

I looked at the scratchings and carved initials on the top of the desk lid.

I found: "J.H. LOVES J.C." And, over it, an unsymmetrical heart pierced by a rather wonky arrow.

But I knew already that J.H. had loved J.C. I had seen the child's face through the window, only this morning—I had seen what did not exist—yet which did exist—

What to do now?

90

My hand, guided, by God knows whom or what, put its fingers into the empty inkwell-socket. The fingers found a closely folded piece of paper.

I unfolded it, carefully, and read:

" 'Dear Mum and Dad, I do not love you. I love Miss Carey. Where she goes, I go. I follow her everywhere. Tonight I have followed her to the school. She has gone to the gymnasium. I shall follow her there. Something is going to happen. That is why I am writing. Whatever she does, I shall do too. Because I love her. I must hurry now, to be with her. Funny really—as she does not even know I follow her! I'll put this under my inkwell. I don't expect you'll ever read it, but you never know. Yours sincerely—Your daughter, Joan.' "

"I didn't know she was there!" cried that voice in my head, loud with its silence. "I didn't know she was there!"

"Of course you didn't!" I answered aloud, loudly. "It's all right! I'll tell them!"

The classroom door opened and Miss Leonard walked in.

"Miss Anderson, what on earth are you doing?"

What on earth was I doing? I was sitting at a dead child's desk, a scrap of paper in my hand, and "talking to myself".

"I've found something, Miss Leonard." I passed her the letter.

She read it. "So *that's* what happened," she said. "Miss Carey didn't take the child there with her at all. The little girl secretly imitated her goddess, even to the point of suicide. Where did you find the letter?"

"In the inkwell-socket. I'm surprised it hasn't been found before, maybe by one of the children."

"No. I cleared that desk myself, removed the inkwell and didn't think to look underneath it. And the children never touch this desk. I did think of removing it, but that's too much like giving in to superstition. What made *you* look there, Miss Anderson?"

"She—she led me here—she spoke in my head—I don't understand it—but it happened—"

"You're psychic, aren't you? Did you know that already?"

"Not until I came to this school."

"You saw her on the day of your interview, didn't you?"

"Yes. On the stairs."

"I remember. And I fobbed you off with a practical explanation."

"Did you ever see her, Miss Leonard."

"No. But Mr. Brown did, more than once. And one of the children, last term, after the fire, insisted that Miss Carey wasn't dead as she'd seen her in the corridor. Neither of them was lying. Some individuals see and hear more than others. Have you been very frightened?"

"At first I wasn't, because I thought she was real. Later, I did feel frightened."

"And now?"

"Now I just feel desperately sorry for her. Her eyes, Miss Leonard. If you could have seen the sadness in her eyes!"

"Mr. Brown mentioned that. You may talk to him if you like, but please no talk of ghosts to anyone else."

"Of course not. Anyway, I think she'll go away now. She'll be free of the place. She's been punished so dreadfully. Maybe ghosts are people in purgatory and we see them around us all the time without realizing that they are ghosts."

"Maybe *you* do," said Miss Leonard, smiling a little.

The bell rang for the beginning of afternoon school. A wail of disappointment rose from outside. I looked out of the window, saw the children cease their snowballing and move obediently towards the building.

Only one figure moved away from the building, moved through the oncoming crowd of girls, who took no notice of her at all. She walked farther away, on and on, past the playground, across the snow-covered playing-field. A pale sun was shining and the snow dazzled, accentuating the thin, dark outline of the woman in black. She looked so utterly alone. Then a small figure began to follow her, running quickly and eagerly, and the sun turned the little figure's mop of red curls into a flame shaped like a rose.

The child overtook the woman in black and walked beside her, lightly, dancingly. And the two retreating figures cast no shadows on the snow, and left no footprints.

A Jug of Syrup

AMBROSE BIERCE

In which old Silas Deemer, who has never missed a day at his shop, dies suddenly. Sometime later, Alvan Creede, a respected citizen, calls at the store and is served a jug of maple syrup by Mr. Deemer himself. But Mr. Creede has forgotten something . . .

THIS narrative begins with the death of its hero. Silas Deemer died on the 16th day of July, 1863, and two days later his remains were buried. As he had been personally known to every man, woman and well-grown child in the village, the funeral, as the local newspaper phrased it, "was largely attended". In accordance with a custom of the time and place, the coffin was opened at the graveside and the entire assembly of friends and neighbours filed past, taking a last look at the face of the dead. And then, before the eyes of all, Silas Deemer was put into the ground. Some of the eyes were a trifle dim, but in a general way it may be said that at that interment there was lack of neither observance nor observation; Silas was indubitably dead, and none could have pointed out any ritual delinquency that would have justified him in coming back from the grave. Yet if human testimony is good for anything (and certainly it once put an end to witchcraft in and about Salem) he came back.

I forgot to state that the death and burial of Silas Deemer occurred in the little village of Hillbrook, where he had lived for thirty-one years. He had been what is known in some parts of the Union (which is admittedly a free country) as a "merchant"; that is to say, he kept a retail shop for the sale of such things as are commonly sold in shops of that character. His honesty had never been questioned, so far as is known, and he was held in high esteem by all. The only thing that could be urged against him by the most censorious was a too close attention to business. It was not urged against him, though many another, who manifested it in no greater degree, was less leniently judged. The business to which Silas was devoted was mostly his own—that, possibly, may have made a difference.

At the time of Deemer's death nobody could recollect a single day, Sundays excepted, that he had not passed in his "store", since he had opened it more than a quarter-century before. His health having been perfect during all that time, he had been unable to discern any validity in whatever may or might have been urged to lure him astray from his counter; and it is related that once when he was summoned to the county seat as a witness in an important law case and did not attend, the lawyer who had the hardihood to move that he be "admonished" was solemnly informed that the Court regarded the proposal with "surprise". Judicial surprise being an emotion that attorneys are not commonly ambitious to arouse, the motion was hastily withdrawn and an agreement with the other side effected as to what Mr. Deemer would have said if he had been there—the other side pushing its advantage to the extreme and making the supposititious testimony distinctly damaging to the interests of its proponents. In brief, it was the general feeling in all that region that Silas Deemer was the one immobile verity of Hillbrook, and that his translation in space would precipitate some dismal public ill or strenuous calamity.

Mrs. Deemer and two grown daughters occupied the upper rooms of the building, but Silas had never been known to sleep elsewhere than on a cot behind the counter of the store. And there, quite by accident, he was found one night, dying, and passed away just before the time for taking down the shutters. Though speechless, he appeared conscious, and it was thought by those who knew him best that if the end had unfortunately been delayed beyond the usual hour for opening the store the effect upon him would have been deplorable.

Such had been Silas Deemer—such the fixity and invariety of his life and habit, that the village humorist (who had once attended college) was moved to bestow upon him the sobriquet of "Old Ibidem", and, in the first issue of the local newspaper after the death, to explain without offence that Silas had taken "a day off".

It was more than a day, but from the record it appears that well within a month Mr. Deemer made it plain that he had not the leisure to be dead.

One of Hillbrook's most respected citizens was Alvan Creede, a banker. He lived in the finest house in town, kept a carriage and was a most estimable man variously. He knew something of the advantages of travel, too, having been frequently in Boston, and once, it was thought, in New York, though he modestly disclaimed that glittering distinction. The matter is mentioned here merely as a contribution to an understanding of Mr. Creede's worth, for either way it is creditable to him—to his intelligence if he had put himself, even temporarily, into contact with metropolitan culture; to his candour if he had not.

One pleasant summer evening at about the hour of ten Mr. Creede, entering at his garden gate, passed up the gravel walk, which looked very white in the moonlight, mounted the stone steps of his fine house and pausing a moment inserted his latchkey in the door. As he pushed this open he met his wife, who was crossing the passage from the parlour to the library.

97

She greeted him pleasantly and pulling the door farther back held it for him to enter. Instead he turned and, looking about his feet in front of the threshold, uttered an exclamation of surprise.

"Why!—what the devil," he said, "has become of that jug?"

"What jug, Alvan?" his wife inquired, not very sympathetically.

"A jug of maple syrup—I brought it along from the store and set it down here to open the door. What the—"

"There, there, Alvan, please don't swear again," said the lady, interrupting. Hillbrook, by the way, is not the only place in Christendom where a vestigial polytheism forbids the taking in vain of the Evil One's name.

The jug of maple syrup which the easy ways of village life had permitted Hillbrook's foremost citizen to carry home from the store was not there.

"Are you quite sure, Alvan?"

"My dear, do you suppose a man does not know when he is carrying a jug? I bought that syrup at Deemer's as I was passing. Deemer himself drew it and lent me the jug, and I—"

The sentence remains to this day unfinished. Mr. Creede staggered into the house, entered the parlour and dropped into an arm-chair, trembling in every limb. He had suddenly remembered that Silas Deemer was three weeks dead.

Mrs. Creede stood by her husband, regarding him with surprise and anxiety.

"For Heaven's sake," she said, "what ails you?"

Mr. Creede's ailment having no obvious relation to the interests of the better land he did not apparently deem it necessary to expound it on that demand; he said nothing—merely stared. There were long moments of silence broken by nothing but the measured ticking of the clock, which seemed somewhat slower than usual, as if it were civilly granting them an extension of time in which to recover their wits.

"Jane, I have gone mad—that is it." He spoke thickly and hurriedly. "You should have told me; you must have observed my symptoms before they became so pronounced that I have observed them myself. I thought I was passing Deemer's store; it was open and lit up—that is what I thought; of course it is never open now. Silas Deemer stood at his desk behind the counter. My God, Jane, I saw him as distinctly as I see you. Remembering that you had said you wanted some maple syrup, I went in and bought some—that is all—I bought two quarts of maple syrup from Silas Deemer, who is dead and underground, but nevertheless drew that syrup from a cask and handed it to me in a jug. He talked with me, too, rather gravely, I remember, even more so than was his way, but not a word of what he said can I now recall. But I saw him—good Lord, I saw and talked with him—and he is dead! So I thought, but I'm mad, Jane, I'm as crazy as a beetle; and you have kept it from me."

This monologue gave the woman time to collect what faculties she had.

"Alvan," she said, "you have given no evidence of insanity, believe me. This was undoubtedly an illusion—how should it be anything else? That would be too terrible! But there is no insanity; you are working too hard at the bank. You should not have attended the meeting of directors this evening; anyone could see that you were ill; I knew something would occur."

It may have seemed to him that the prophecy had lagged a bit, awaiting the event, but he said nothing of that, being concerned with his own condition. He was calm now, and could think coherently.

"Doubtless the phenomenon was subjective," he said, with a somewhat ludicrous transition to the slang of science. "Granting the possibility of spiritual apparition and even materialization, yet the apparition and materialization of a half-gallon brown clay jug—a piece of coarse, heavy pottery evolved from nothing—that is hardly thinkable."

As he finished speaking, a child ran into the room—his little daughter. She was clad in a bedgown. Hastening to her father she threw her arms about his neck, saying: "You naughty papa, you forgot to come in and kiss me. We heard you open the gate and got up and looked out. And, papa dear, Eddy says mayn't he have the little jug when it is empty?"

As the full import of that revelation imparted itself to Alvan Creede's understanding he visibly shuddered. For the child could not have heard a word of the conversation.

The estate of Silas Deemer being in the hands of an administrator who had thought it best to dispose of the "business", the store had been closed ever since the owner's death, the goods having been removed by another "merchant" who had purchased them *en bloc*. The rooms above were vacant as well, for the widow and daughters had gone to another town.

On the evening immediately after Alvan Creede's adventure (which had somehow "got out") a crowd of men, women and children thronged the sidewalk opposite the store. That the place was haunted by the spirit of the late Silas Deemer was now well known to every resident of Hillbrook, though many affected disbelief. Of these the hardiest, and in a general way the youngest, threw stones against the front of the building, the only part accessible, but carefully missed the unshuttered windows. Incredulity had not grown to malice. A few venturesome souls crossed the street and rattled the door in its frame; struck matches and held them near the window;

100

attempted to view the black interior. Some of the spectators invited attention to their wit by shouting and groaning and challenging the ghost to a foot-race.

After a considerable time had elapsed without any manifestation, and many of the crowd had gone away, all those remaining began to observe that the interior of the store was suffused with a dim, yellow light. At this all demonstrations ceased; the intrepid souls about the door and windows fell back to the opposite side of the street and were merged in the crowd; the small boys ceased throwing stones. Nobody spoke above his breath; all whispered excitedly and pointed to the now steadily growing light. How long a time had passed since the first faint glow had been observed none could have guessed, but eventually the illumination was bright enough to reveal the whole interior of the store; and there, standing at his desk behind the counter Silas Deemer was distinctly visible!

The effect upon the crowd was marvellous. It began rapidly to melt away at both flanks, as the timid left the place. Many ran as fast as their legs would let them; others moved off with greater dignity, turning occasionally to look backward over the shoulder. At last a score or more, mostly men, remained where they were, speechless, staring, excited. The apparition inside gave them no attention; it was apparently occupied with a book of accounts.

Presently three men left the crowd on the sidewalk as if by a common impulse and crossed the street. One of them, a heavy man, was about to set his shoulder against the door when it opened, apparently without human agency, and the courageous investigators passed in. No sooner had they crossed the threshold than they were seen by the awed observers outside to be acting in the most unaccountable way. They thrust out their hands before them, pursued devious courses, came into violent

collision with the counter, with boxes and barrels on the floor, and with one another. They turned awkwardly hither and thither and seemed trying to escape, but unable to retrace their steps. Their voices were heard in exclamations and curses. But in no way did the apparition of Silas Deemer manifest an interest in what was going on.

By what impulse the crowd was moved none ever recollected, but the entire mass—men, women, children, dogs—made a simultaneous and tumultuous rush for the entrance. They congested the doorway, pushing for precedence—resolving themselves at length into a line and moving up step by step. By some subtle spiritual or physical alchemy observation had been transmuted into action—the sightseers had become parti- cipants in the spectacle—the audience had usurped the stage.

To the only spectator remaining on the other side of the street—Alvan Creede, the banker—the interior of the store with its inpouring crowd continued in full illumination; all the strange things going on there were clearly visible. To those inside all was black darkness. It was as if each person as he was thrust in at the door had been stricken blind, and was maddened by the mischance. They groped with aimless imprecision, tried to force their way out against the current, pushed and elbowed, struck at random, fell and were trampled, rose and trampled in their turn. They seized one another by the garments, the hair, the beard—fought like animals, cursed, shouted, called one another opprobrious and obscene names. When, finally, Alvan Creede had seen the last person of the line pass into that awful tumult the light that had illuminated it was suddenly quenched and all was as black to him as to those within. He turned away and left the place.

In the early morning a curious crowd had gathered about "Deemer's". It was composed partly of those who had run away

103

the night before, but now had the courage of sunshine, partly of honest folk going to their daily toil. The door of the store stood open; the place was vacant, but on the walls, the floor, the furniture, were shreds of clothing and tangles of hair. Hillbrook militant had managed somehow to pull itself out and had gone home to medicine its hurts and swear that it had been all night in bed. On the dusty desk, behind the counter, was the sales book. The entries in it, in Deemer's handwriting had ceased on the 16th day of July, the last of his life. There was no record of a later sale to Alvan Creede.

That is the entire story—except that men's passions having subsided and reason having resumed its immemorial sway, it was confessed in Hillbrook that, considering the harmless and honourable character of his first commercial transaction under the new conditions, Silas Deemer, deceased, might properly have been suffered to resume business at the old stand without mobbing. In that judgment the local historian from whose unpublished work these facts are compiled had the thoughtfulness to signify his concurrence.

The Open Window

SAKI

In which Mr. Nuttel pays a call on Mrs. Sappleton, and is greeted by her young niece, who tells him of her aunt's great tragedy. Three years ago her husband and two brothers were lost shooting on the moors, and Mrs. Sappleton keeps the french windows open every evening until dusk in the hope they will come back.

"MY aunt will be down presently, Mr. Nuttel," said a very self-possessed young lady of fifteen; "in the meantime you must try and put up with me."

Framton Nuttel endeavoured to say the correct something which should duly flatter the niece of the moment without unduly discounting the aunt that was to come. Privately he doubted more than ever whether these formal visits on a succession of total strangers would do much towards helping the nerve cure which he was supposed to be undergoing.

"I know how it will be," his sister had said when he was preparing to migrate to this rural retreat; "you will bury yourself down there and not speak to a living soul, and your nerves will be worse than ever from moping. I shall just give you letters of introduction to all the people I know there. Some of them, as far as I can remember, were quite nice."

Framton wondered whether Mrs. Sappleton, the lady to

whom he was presenting one of the letters of introduction, came into the nice division.

"Do you know many of the people round here?" asked the niece, when she judged that they had had sufficient silent communion.

"Hardly a soul," said Framton. "My sister was staying here, at the rectory, you know, some four years ago, and she gave me letters of introduction to some of the people here."

He made the last statement in a tone of distinct regret.

"Then you know practically nothing about *my* aunt?" pursued the self-possessed young lady.

"Only her name and address," admitted the caller. He was wondering whether Mrs. Sappleton was in the married or the widowed state. An undefinable something about the room seemed to suggest masculine habitation.

"Her great tragedy happened just three years ago," said the child; "that would be since your sister's time."

"Her tragedy?" asked Framton; somehow in this restful country spot tragedies seemed out of place.

"You may wonder why we keep that window wide open on an October afternoon," said the niece, indicating a large french window that opened on to a lawn.

"It is quite warm for the time of the year," said Framton; "but has that window got anything to do with the tragedy?"

"Out through that window, three years ago to a day, her husband and her two young brothers went off for their day's shooting. They never came back. In crossing the moor to their favourite snipe-shooting ground they were all three engulfed in a treacherous piece of bog. It had been that dreadful wet summer, you know, and places that were safe in other years gave way suddenly without warning. Their bodies were never recovered. That was the dreadful part of it." Here the child's voice lost its

106

self-possessed note and became falteringly human. "Poor Aunt always thinks that they will come back some day, they and the little brown spaniel that was lost with them, and walk in at that window just as they used to do. That is why the window is kept open every evening till it is quite dusk. Poor dear Aunt, she has often told me how they went out, her husband with his white waterproof over his arm, and Ronnie, her youngest brother, singing, 'Bertie, why do you bound?' as he always did to tease her, because she said it got on her nerves. Do you know, sometimes on still, quiet evenings like this, I almost get a creepy feeling that they *will* walk in through that window—"

She broke off with a little shudder. It was a relief to Framton when the aunt bustled into the room with a whirl of apologies for being late in making her appearance.

"I hope Vera has been amusing you?" she said.

"She has been very interesting," said Framton.

"I hope you don't mind the open window," said Mrs. Sappleton briskly; "my husband and brothers will be home directly from shooting, and they always come in this way. They've been out for snipe in the marshes today, so they'll make a fine mess over my poor carpets. So like you menfolk, isn't it?"

She rattled on cheerfully about the shooting and the scarcity of birds, and the prospects for duck in the winter. To Framton it was all purely horrible. He made a desperate but only partially successful effort to turn the talk on to a less ghastly topic; he was conscious that his hostess was giving him only a fragment of her attention, and her eyes were constantly straying past him to the open window and the lawn beyond. It was certainly an unfortunate coincidence that he should have paid his visit on this tragic anniversary.

"The doctors agree in ordering me complete rest, an absence

107

of mental excitement, and avoidance of anything in the nature of violent physical exercise," announced Framton, who laboured under the tolerably wide-spread delusion that total strangers and chance acquaintances are hungry for the least detail of one's ailments and infirmities, their cause and cure. "On the matter of diet they are not so much in agreement," he continued.

"No?" said Mrs. Sappleton, in a voice which only replaced a yawn at the last moment. Then she suddenly brightened into alert attention—but not to what Framton was saying.

"Here they are at last!" she cried. "Just in time for tea, and don't they look as if they were muddy up to the eyes!"

Framton shivered slightly and turned towards the niece with a look intended to convey sympathetic comprehension. The child was staring out through the open window with dazed horror in her eyes. In a chill shock of nameless fear Framton swung round in his seat and looked in the same direction.

In the deepening twilight three figures were walking across the lawn towards the window; they all carried guns under their arms, and one of them was additionally burdened with a white coat hung over his shoulders. A tired brown spaniel kept close at their heels. Noiselessly they neared the house, and then a hoarse young voice chanted out of the dusk: "I said, Bertie, why do you bound?"

Framton grabbed wildly at his stick and hat; the hall door, the gravel-drive, and the front gate were dimly noted stages in his headlong retreat. A cyclist coming along the road had to run into the hedge to avoid imminent collision.

"Here we are, my dear," said the bearer of the white mackintosh, coming in through the window; "fairly muddy, but most of it's dry. Who was that who bolted out as we came up?"

"A most extraordinary man, a Mr. Nuttel," said Mrs. Sappleton; "could only talk about his illnesses, and dashed off without a word of good-bye or apology when you arrived. One would think he had seen a ghost."

"I expect it was the spaniel," said the niece calmly; "he told me he had a horror of dogs. He was once hunted into a cemetery somewhere on the banks of the Ganges by a pack of pariah dogs, and had to spend the night in a newly dug grave with the creatures snarling and grinning and foaming just above him. Enough to make anyone lose their nerve."

Romance at short notice was her speciality.

The Old Wife and the Ghost

JAMES REEVES

THERE was an old wife and she lived all alone
 In a cottage not far from Hitchin:
And one bright night, by the full moon light,
 Comes a ghost right into her kitchen.

About that kitchen neat and clean
 The ghost goes pottering round.
But the poor old wife is deaf as a boot
 And so hears never a sound.

The ghost blows up the kitchen fire,
 As bold as bold can be;
He helps himself from the larder shelf,
 But never a sound hears she.

He blows on his hands to make them warm,
 And whistles aloud "Whee-hee!"
But still as a sack the old soul lies
 And never a sound hears she.

From corner to corner he runs about,
 And into the cupboard he peeps;
He rattles the door and bumps on the floor,
 But still the old wife sleeps.

Jangle and bang go the pots and pans,
  As he throws them all around;
And the plates and mugs and dishes and jugs,
  He flings them all to the ground.

Madly the ghost tears up and down
  And screams like a storm at sea;
And at last the old wife stirs in her bed—
  And it's "Drat those mice," says she.

Then the first cock crows and morning shows
  And the troublesome ghost's away.
But oh! what a pickle the poor wife sees
  When she gets up next day.

"Them's tidy big mice," the old wife thinks,
  And off she goes to Hitchin,
And a tidy big cat she fetches back
  To keep the mice from her kitchen.

The Wild Ride in the Tilt Cart

SORCHE NIC LEODHAS

In which Tommy Hayes arrives in the Scottish Highlands for a fishing holiday with his friend. There is no one to meet him at the station, so he sets out to walk the lonely five miles at night. An old tilt cart comes by and slows down to give Tommy a lift . . .

THERE was a lad named Tommy Hayes and a more likeable lad you'd never hope to see, for all that he was a Sassenach born and bred. Tommy was the sort to take his fishing very seriously, so when a Scottish friend wrote him and invited him to come up to his place in the Highlands for a visit and be sure to bring his fishing gear, Tommy was delighted. He'd always heard the fishing up where his friend lived was extra fine but he'd never had a chance to try it before. So right away he sent a telegram to his friend to say he was coming and what time they could expect him to get there. Then he packed up his fishing gear and a few clothes in his bag, and off he went.

He stepped off the train just about nightfall into the midst of a teeming rain with the water coming down in bucketsful and sloshing all over the place. The very first thing he discovered was that nobody had come to meet him. The station was on the edge of a small village, and there wasn't a soul in sight except for

114

the stationmaster, and he was inside the station keeping out of the rain.

Tommy couldn't understand it for he'd sent the telegram in plenty of time. He went in and asked the stationmaster if he had seen anyone in the village from his friend's place, thinking maybe they'd had an errand to do and would be coming along for him later. But the stationmaster said that nobody at all had come over from that way for as good as a week. Tommy was surprised and maybe a little bit annoyed but he settled down in a corner of the station to wait for somebody to come and fetch him. He waited and waited and waited but nobody came at all, and after a while he found out why. The stationmaster came out of his bit of an office with a telegram in his hand. "This is for the folks up where you're going," he told Tommy. "Maybe you'd not mind taking it along, since you're going there yourself."

Tommy didn't have to read the telegram to know that it was the one he had sent to his friend. Well, that explained why nobody had come to meet his train. And what was more, nobody was going to come. Since the telegram hadn't been delivered, they wouldn't know at all that he was there.

"Och, well, 'tis a pity," said the stationmaster. " 'Twas early this morn I got it, and I'd have sent it along had anyone been passing by that was going in that direction. But what with the weather and all, there's few been out this day, and what there was, was bound the other way."

Well, being a good-natured lad, Tommy couldn't see any sense in making a fuss about it. He'd just have to find a way for himself to get where he wanted to go.

The stationmaster was sorry for Tommy, but he could give him no help. There was nobody in the village who'd be able to take Tommy to his friend's house that night. Two or three of the folks had farm carts, but the beasts were all put up for the night and folks were all in their beds. They wouldn't be likely to take it kindly if Tommy woke them out of their sleep.

"You could stay in the station o'ernight," the man said. "You'd be welcome to do so, if you liked to. Happen there'll be someone along on the morrow going the way you want to go."

"And maybe not," said Tommy, not feeling very hopeful. "No, if I'm going to get there at all, I can see I'll have to walk."

"Aye," the stationmaster agreed. " 'Tis a matter of five miles."

"That's not too bad," said Tommy, determined to be cheerful.

"Mostly up and down hill," said the stationmaster glumly. "The road is rough, forbye. And 'tis raining."

"It can't be helped," said Tommy. "I'll just have to make the best of it." He picked up his bag and started out into the rain. The stationmaster came to the door and pointed out the road Tommy was to take. Tommy had gone a little way when the man called out after him. "Have a care for auld Rabbie MacLaren! I doubt he'll be out on the road the night."

That didn't mean a thing to Tommy, so he just plodded along through the rain.

The stationmaster had told him no lies about the road. Tommy couldn't remember having trod a worse one. It was up and down hill all right. Tommy toiled along, splashing through the puddles and slipping on loose pebbles with the rain pouring from the back of his hat brim down inside the collar of his coat. He was beginning to wonder if the fishing was going to be fine enough to pay for all the trouble he was going through to get it when he heard the sound of cart wheels rolling up the hill behind him.

He stopped and turned to look, and although it was growing dark he could make out the vague shape of a tilt cart coming

116

toward him. It had a canvas top stretched over some sort of a framework, and Tommy thought to himself that if he could get a lift he'd be out of the rain at any rate. He set his bag down and stood in the middle of the road, waving his arms and shouting.

"Will you give me a lift up the road?" called Tommy.

The driver did not answer but the cart came on swiftly, bumping along over the ruts in a heedless way. As it came up to him, Tommy called out again. "Will you give me a lift?"

The man in the cart didn't say "Aye," but he didn't say "Nay." The cart kept on rolling along and Tommy had to pick up his bag and jump to the side of the road to keep from being run down.

"I'll pay you well," cried Tommy as he jumped. He felt rather desperate. The tilt cart was his only hope, for he doubted if he'd have another chance to get a lift that night. "I'll pay you well!" said Tommy again.

The driver did not answer, but it seemed to Tommy that the horse that was drawing the cart slowed down a little. Tommy took that as a sign that his offer had been accepted. He picked up his bag and ran after the cart and hopped in beside the driver without waiting for the cart to come to a full stop.

As soon as Tommy was in the cart the horse picked up speed again. The creature didn't seem to be minding the roughness of the road in the least. It brought the cart up to the crest of the hill at a good round pace and, when they started down the other side, the horse stretched its legs and fairly flew. The cart bounced and bumped and jolted over the ruts and Tommy's teeth chattered with the shaking he was getting. All he could do was hold fast to the side of the cart and hope for the best. The cart wheels threw out sparks as they hit the stones that strewed the road, and every now and then a big one sent the cart a foot or more in the air. Uphill and downhill went Tommy with the cart, hanging on for dear life and expecting to land any minute in a heap in the ditch with horse, cart, and driver piled on top of him.

He plucked up enough courage after a while to attempt to implore the driver to slow down. He turned to look at the man beside him. What he saw took the words out of his mouth. It wasn't so much the sight of him, although that was bad enough. He was the hairiest creature Tommy had seen in his life. A wild thatch of hair grew over his head and down over his ears, and was met by a long grizzled beard that almost covered his face and blew in the wind as if it had life of its own. But that wasn't what struck Tommy dumb. With all that hair in the way Tommy could not be sure of it, yet he'd have sworn the man was grinning at him. Tommy didn't like it. He felt that grin was full of a peculiar sort of evil, and it gave Tommy such a queer feeling that he hurriedly turned away without saying a word.

Just at that moment the road made a turn and he saw at the side of it, a little distance ahead, a great stone gateway. Tommy knew from the stationmaster's description that it was the entrance to his friend's place.

He gave a great sigh of relief. "Pull up!" he cried to the driver. "This is where I get out."

But the driver made no sign of stopping, and the horse went racing past the gate. Tommy rose in his seat, shouting, "Stop!" Just then the cartwheels hit some obstruction in the road and Tommy, taken unawares, lost his balance. Over the side of the cart he flew and landed in the road on his hands and knees. By the time he pulled himself together and got to his feet, the cart was out of sight, although he could still hear the horse's hooves pounding down the other side of the hill.

Tommy would have liked to have had a chance to tell the fellow exactly what he thought of him, but it was too late for

that. The cart was gone, and Tommy's bag had gone with it, but at least he hadn't paid the driver. Taking what comfort he could from that, Tommy limped back to the gateway, and up the drive to the door of his friend's house.

Tommy's friend was terribly surprised when he opened the door at Tommy's knock, and saw him standing there on the doorstone. But when he saw the plight Tommy was in he asked no questions. He hurried Tommy up to his room and saw that he had a good hot bath and found him some dry clothes to put on.

When Tommy came downstairs again, warm and dry and feeling a hundred times better, he was so relieved to have arrived safely that he was prepared to treat his whole experience as a joke. He handed over the telegram and told his friend he didn't think much of the telegraph service in the Highlands.

Tommy's friend had several other guests staying with him and they all gathered around Tommy now to hear the story of his mishap.

"Och, Tommy lad," said his friend. " 'Tis a long road and a bad night for walking."

"Did you walk all the way?" asked one of the guests.

"Well, no," said Tommy. "But I wish that I had. I got a lift from one of your wild Highlanders. I never had such a ride in my life before and I hope that I never shall again. And to top it all, the fellow went off with my bag."

"I wonder who it would be?" asked Tommy's friend. "Not many would be travelling in weather the like of this at night. The road is bad enough at best. A bit of rain makes it terrible."

"I'll grant you that," said Tommy. "The fellow was driving a tilt cart."

"A tilt cart!" exclaimed another man. "Och, they're none so common hereabouts. The only one I call to mind is the one belonging to auld Rabbie MacLaren."

"Now that you mention it, I remember," said Tommy. "That was the name of the man the stationmaster told me to have a care for. I suppose he meant that I was to keep out of his way. How I wish I had!"

There was a dead silence for all of five minutes. Then Tommy's friend asked, "What sort of man was he to look at, Tommy?"

"An old man, I'd say," Tommy told him. "He had more hair on his head and face than I've ever seen on a human being before. It probably looked like more than there really was of it, because it was so tangled and matted. Of course it was too dark for me to see much of him."

"What was the horse like, Tommy?" asked his friend.

"Not what you'd call a big beast," Tommy answered. "In fact he was somewhat on the small side. But how he could go! That horse would make a fortune on a race track. We bumped and thumped along at such a pace that I expected both wheels to fly off at any minute."

" 'Twas auld Rabbie MacLaren, to be sure!" said the guest who had asked about the tilt cart. "He was always one to be driving as if the de'il himself was after him. There's a bad spot a mile further on, over the hill. If you miss the road on the turn there, over the cliff you go to the glen below. Auld Rabbie came tearing along hell-bent one stormy night and missed the turn and went over."

"Went over!" Tommy exclaimed. "It's a wonder he wasn't killed!"

"Killed?" repeated the other man. "Of course he was killed. Auld Rabbie's been dead for a dozen years."

It took Tommy a minute or two to get through his head what he was being told. Then all of a sudden he understood.

"Dead!" screeched Tommy. *"Then I've been riding with a ghost!"* and he fainted dead away.

The next morning one of the gillies brought Tommy's bag up to the house to see if it belonged to anyone there. He'd found it lying in the glen at the foot of the cliff, below the road. It was the good stout sort of bag that is strapped as well as locked, so all the harm that had come to it was a scratch here and there.

Tommy had recovered from his fright by that time, so they took him out and showed him the place where auld Rabbie went over. They told Tommy he was lucky that he left the cart where he did, for when it got to the bad spot the tragedy was always re-enacted and over the cliff again went the old man with his cart and his horse. There had been some folks who got a ride with auld Rabbie, expecting to reach the village over beyond the next hill, who had found themselves below the road in the glen instead. A number of them had been badly hurt, and two or three had never lived to tell the tale.

Tommy suffered no ill effects from his experience. To tell the truth, he was rather proud of it. And as he took his fishing seriously, he didn't let the ride with auld Rabbie spoil his holiday. He stayed on to the end and fished all the streams in the neighbourhood, and had a wonderful time.

But for a long time after he went home to London he couldn't sleep well on stormy nights. As soon as he turned out the light and closed his eyes he started to dream that he was riding wildly over that rough stony road in the tilt cart with the ghost of auld Rabbie MacLaren.

Old Wine in New Bottles

JOHN EDGELL

In which Jacob Strauss suffers delusions of being followed. His doctor says he is overworked and recommends that he take a holiday. After three peaceful days in Paris Strauss flies to New York and books into a quiet hotel in Manhattan. The first night he wakes suddenly and feels that someone is in his room . . .

WHEN Jacob Strauss knew that something was very wrong with him, his first reaction was to visit his doctor. He went to the surgery, read magazines in the waiting-room, and then his turn came. The doctor was sitting behind a large desk, fingering his moustache.

"Well, Mr. Strauss, what can I do for you?"

Jacob Strauss sat down.

"I haven't been feeling well," he said.

"Naturally," said the doctor. "Can't you be more specific?"

"This may sound strange to you," Jacob said, "but I get the odd feeling that I am being followed around."

"Followed around?" The doctor scribbled something on his pad.

"Yes. The feeling that someone is walking behind me. That's the only way I can explain it. If I had eyes in the back of my head

I'd be able to see whoever it is. But when I turn round, even when I turn round very quickly, I can't see anything strange."

"Do you work hard?" the doctor asked, taking off his spectacles.

"Yes."

"Why don't you have a holiday? Get away from it all. Take three weeks, and go and lie in the sun. If that doesn't cure you, come back and I'll see what I can do then."

Jacob Strauss went home. He lived alone in a room at the top of an old-fashioned lodging house. It wasn't a very attractive room, but his work called for a lot of travelling and there didn't seem to be any sense in having an expensive home.

He lay down on the bed. Perhaps the doctor was right. He hadn't had a holiday for two years and he *had* been working hard recently. Too hard. He laughed to himself. He had first felt that he was being followed about a month ago when, late at night, he had been returning to his room after a visit to the cinema. It had been a strange sensation. He had felt that someone was walking behind him, watching him, eyes burning into his back. But when he had turned round, there was not a soul in sight. What struck Jacob most was the very realness of the feeling. In his heart of hearts, he *knew* someone had been following him.

A few days later the same thing had happened again, only this time he had been in his own room. He was looking out of the window when, all of a sudden, he sensed the presence of someone else, someone whose eyes pierced his back. Jacob had turned round, but apart from himself the room was empty.

Now, lying on the bed, he felt that he could laugh at himself. The doctor was right. It was simply overwork, nothing more.

The very next morning he telephoned his secretary and told her that he was taking a holiday on his doctor's orders. He went

124

to a travel agency and arranged to catch a train that night to take him to Paris. After Paris he might fly to New York, but he didn't want to fix any definite plans. If he was going to have a holiday, he might just as well feel free.

The train journey was uneventful. He had a sleeping compartment and slept soundly, waking only when the steward called him for breakfast. The steward was German like himself.

"On holiday, sir?" he asked.

Jacob said, "Getting away from it all."

He spent three days in Paris, walking by the River Seine, enjoying the spring sunshine and the feeling that he was getting better. Free from the strain of his work, he was completely relaxed. On his last day in Paris he booked a seat on the morning flight to New York. He had never been to the United States and was looking forward to the trip with some anticipation.

He slept badly that night, perhaps because he was excited about the flight in the morning. When he woke the candystripe bedsheets were twisted, and some were lying across the floor, as if he had been moving about a great deal in his sleep. But he could not remember having dreamed; when he did dream he usually remembered it quite clearly in the morning.

On the flight to New York he slept most of the way, waking only when lunch was being served. He enjoyed the sensation of the plane, soaring like a great mechanical bird thousands of feet above the ocean. If the plane were to crash, Jacob thought, it would drop into the ocean and sink like a stone. But it didn't crash, thankfully, and arrived in New York exactly on schedule.

Jacob booked into a hotel in Manhattan. It wasn't an expensive place, since he couldn't afford one, but the service was good and the food, although a little unusual, was pleasant. That first night in New York, tired by the long flight, he fell asleep at once.

He woke suddenly sometime early in the morning. His room was on the twelfth floor and he was conscious of the very quiet traffic sounds, the whisper of cars, that drifted up to him. A neon light, flashing from across the street, blinked against the wall of his room. Jacob sat up. Why had he woken?

He had woken because, out of the furthest corner of his eye, he had seen someone in the room. He reached out and turned on the bedside light. But the room was empty. It was an ordinary hotel room. There was no-one in it but himself.

He lay down again, sweating, but did not turn the light off this time. He stared up at the ceiling. Could it be true? Even here, in New York, thousands of miles from Hamburg, could he still be imagining that he was being followed? He did not sleep again for a long time. The first light of dawn streaked the sky before sleep fitfully came again.

When he awoke in the morning he ate his doughnut and drank his coffee very quickly, and left the hotel. He walked around the streets of Manhattan, looking at the Empire State Building and other sights and listening to the unfamiliar sounds. He behaved like any ordinary tourist, but something was gnawing at the back of his mind.

He took his lunch in a small restaurant near Central Park and was about to pay the bill when he became conscious of someone staring at him from behind. This time he thought the best thing was to ignore the feeling, to pretend that it did not exist, but still he could not prevent a quick backward glance.

He noticed a shadow moving in the darkened corner between the curtain and the window. It looked like a shadow thrown by a human being, but there was no-one near who could have thrown it. Jacob felt a little sick. Had he imagined it; or had he caught his first glimpse of "the thing" that followed his every footstep?

126

He hurried out into the street. Walking along through the lunchtime crowds he could not shake off the feeling that he was being pursued through the streets. Nervously he glanced behind him, but all he could see were crowds of fixed and unfamiliar faces. The "thing" was invisible.

He went back to his hotel. In his room he locked the door and sat down in a chair by the window. What did it all mean, he wondered. Was he going mad? Or was there really ... *something* ... following him? He looked down into Third Avenue far below. He had always been a calm, reasonable man. He worked hard, certainly, but he had always thought that his nerves were good and that he could stand any kind of strain. But this whole business was beginning to terrify him.

Later in the afternoon he left his room again. He nearly forgot his key. He stepped into the elevator and pressed the button for the ground floor. Although he was quite alone in the front of the lift, he had the overpowering feeling that someone was standing immediately behind him. When he turned to look he noticed a shadow against the wall. It was his own shadow, it could only be his own shadow, since there was no-one else in the lift.

But it was not connected at the feet.

It was a different shape; the nose was longer, the shoulders rounder, and the body was thinner than his own. He felt a growing sense of terror. The shadow drifted to the opposite wall.

When the lift reached the ground floor he stepped out quickly and hurried through the foyer. The clerk at the desk called to him.

"Mr. Strauss? There's a message for you."

"For me?" Jacob asked, surprised. He did not know anyone in America and so far as he knew he had told no-one of his trip.

The clerk handed him an envelope. "You're Mr. Strauss,

127

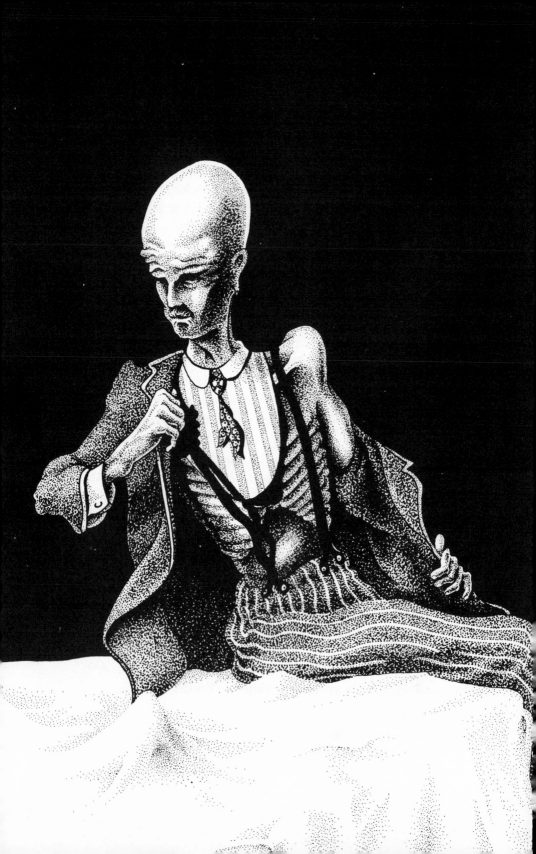

aren't you? Room 1214?"

Jacob took the envelope and opened it. It contained a slip of paper which read, "Old wine in new bottles". He tore the paper up and walked on to the street. He mixed and bumped with the afternoon crowds but even amongst so many people he could not feel safe. He felt exposed to a terrible danger, and began to fear a heart attack. What did the message mean? Was he the old wine or a new bottle? He couldn't stop to think. He kept walking, the terror growing inside him until his blood felt dry. He only knew that he was afraid, truly afraid, for the first time in his life. The shadow knew it, too.

At around five o'clock he went into a darkened bar near Broadway for a drink to steady his nerves. He sat at the counter and drank a glass of whisky. Some minutes later he sensed someone sitting at his elbow and he turned to look.

Beside him was a very old man in an old-fashioned black frock coat. He was staring dimly at Jacob, as if from afar.

"Did you get my message?" he asked, at length.

The old man tapped his fingers on the table, but no sound came.

"What do you want from me?" Jacob asked in fear. His hands were shaking.

"I first saw you in Hamburg, just after I died. I've been following you around ever since. You certainly travel, don't you?" The old man suddenly sounded exhausted. "It was hard to keep up with you."

Jacob looked at him: his flesh was pale, translucent, like old parchment drawn across bleached bones. He might have been a hundred years old. The barman did not seem to see him.

"What do you want from me?" Jacob trembled.

The barman addressed Jacob. "Is everything all right, sir?"

"Ignore the barman, as he ignores me," said the old man.

"Yes—yes—give me another whisky," said Jacob. As the barman poured the drink, the old man seemed to begin struggling, but his efforts were to no avail. In a few seconds, Jacob could literally see right through his body. The shadow said:

"Remember to forgive me..." A moment later, the shape had vanished; the bar stool was empty, and the seat was covered with bits of dust.

Jacob swallowed his whisky, and staggered out into the sunlight.

He felt very cold and tired. Suppose that he was imagining the whole thing? Just suppose ... Then he was sicker than he had realised.

He returned to his hotel room and lay down on the bed; he fell asleep for a time. When he woke, dawn was lifting the empty sky. At the foot of his bed, he saw the old man. His body was a shadow through which the grey light of day shone like a feeble mist.

"Hello, Jacob," it said, slowly removing the frock coat.

Jacob opened his mouth to scream, before he was immersed in the awful blackness he had always known would come.

The decomposing body of an old man was found lying next morning in Jacob Strauss's bed. The doctor said he was at least ninety years old, and had been dead for some time. Jacob's clothes hung in the wardrobe. The hotel manager could not understand it and the police did not bother to investigate. There were too many unsolved puzzles. Of Jacob Strauss nothing was heard again, although the hotel doorman reported seeing a man who looked very like him hurrying from the building early that morning. He had been wearing an old frock coat.

*   *   *

If you ever have the feeling of being followed, it could, of course, be your imagination.

But it might be something else.

The Inexperienced Ghost

— — — — — — — — — — — — — — — —

H. G. WELLS

In which Clayton meets a ghost at the Mermaid Club, where he is staying overnight. But this is rather an odd ghost, his physique and attitude are so weak—not in the least frightening. When he comes face to face with Clayton, he meets with astonishing difficulties . . .

THE scene amidst which Clayton told his last story comes back very vividly to my mind. There he sat, for the greater part of the time, in the corner of the authentic settle by the spacious open fire, and Sanderson sat beside him smoking the Broseley clay pipe that bore his name. There was Evans, and that marvel among actors, Wish, who is also a modest man. We had all come down to the Mermaid Club that Saturday morning, except Clayton, who had slept there overnight—which indeed gave him the opening of his story. We had golfed until golfing was invisible; we had dined, and we were in that mood of tranquil kindliness when men will suffer a story. When Clayton began to tell one, we naturally supposed he was lying. It may be that indeed he was lying—of that the reader will speedily be able to judge as well as I. He began, it is true, with an air of matter-of-fact anecdote, but that we thought was only the incurable artifice of the man.

"I say!" he remarked, after a long consideration of the upward rain of sparks from the log that Sanderson had thumped, "you know I was alone here last night?"

"Except for the domestics," said Wish.

"Who sleep in the other wing," said Clayton. "Yes. Well—" He pulled at his cigar for some little time as though he still hesitated about his confidence. Then he said, quite quietly, "I caught a ghost!"

"Caught a ghost, did you?" said Sanderson. "Where is it?"

And Evans, who admires Clayton immensely, and has been four weeks in America, shouted, "*Caught* a ghost, did you, Clayton? I'm glad of it! Tell us all about it right now."

Clayton said he would in a minute, and asked him to shut the door.

He looked apologetically at me. "There's no eavesdropping, of course, but we don't want to upset our very excellent service with any rumours of ghosts in the place. There's too much shadow and oak panelling to trifle with that. And this, you know, wasn't a regular ghost. I don't think it will come again—ever."

"You mean to say you didn't keep it?" said Sanderson.

"I hadn't the heart to," said Clayton.

And Sanderson said he was surprised.

We laughed, and Clayton looked aggrieved. "I know," he said, with the flicker of a smile, "but the fact is it really *was* a ghost, and I'm as sure of it as I am that I am talking to you now. I'm not joking. I mean what I say."

Sanderson drew deeply at his pipe, with one reddish eye on Clayton, and then emitted a thin jet of smoke more eloquent than many words.

Clayton ignored the comment. "It is the strangest thing that has ever happened in my life. You know I never believed in ghosts or anything of the sort, before, ever; and then, you know, I bag one in a corner; and the whole business is in my hands."

133

He meditated still more profoundly and produced and began to pierce a second cigar with a curious little stabber he affected.

"You talked to it?" asked Wish.

"For the space, probably, of an hour."

"Chatty?" I said, joining the party of the sceptics.

"The poor devil was in trouble," said Clayton, bowed over his cigar-end, and with the very faintest note of reproof. "Sobbing, in fact."

"Sobbing?" someone asked.

Clayton heaved a realistic sigh at the memory. "Good Lord!" he said; "yes." And then, "Poor fellow! yes."

"Where did you strike it?" asked Evans, in his best American accent.

"I never realised," said Clayton, ignoring him, "the poor sort of thing a ghost might be," and he hung us up again for a time, while he sought for matches in his pocket and lit and warmed to his cigar.

"I took an advantage," he reflected at last.

We were none of us in a hurry. "A character", he said, "remains just the same character, for all that it's been disembodied. That's a thing we too often forget. People with a certain strength or fixity of purpose may have ghosts of a certain strength and fixity of purpose—most haunting ghosts, you know, must be as one-idea'd as monomaniacs, and as obstinate as mules, to come back again and again. This poor creature wasn't." He suddenly looked up rather queerly, and his eye went round the room. "I say it", he said, "in all kindliness, but that is the plain truth of the case. Even at the first glance he struck me as weak."

He punctuated with the help of his cigar.

"I came upon him, you know, in the long passage. His back was towards me, and I saw him first. Right off I knew him for a ghost. He was transparent, and whitish; clean through his chest I could see the glimmer of the little window at the end. And not only his physique, but his attitude, struck me as being weak. He looked, you know, as though he didn't know in the slightest whatever he meant to do. One hand was on the panelling and the other fluttered to his mouth. Like—*so!*"

"What sort of physique?" said Sanderson.

"Lean. You know that sort of young man's neck that has two great flutings down the back, here and here—so! And a little, meanish head with scrubby hair and rather bad ears. Shoulders bad, narrower than the hips; turndown collar, ready-made short jacket, trousers baggy and a little frayed at the heels. That's how he took me. I came very quietly up the staircase. I did not carry a light, you know—the candles are on the landing table, and there is that lamp—and I was in my felt slippers, and I saw him as I came up. I stopped dead at that—taking him in. I wasn't a bit afraid. I think that in most of these affairs one is never nearly so afraid or excited as one imagines one would be. I was surprised and interested. I thought, 'Good Lord! Here's a ghost at last! And I haven't believed for a moment in ghosts during the last five-and-twenty years'."

"Um," said Wish.

"I suppose I wasn't on the landing a moment before he found out I was there. He turned on me sharply, and I saw the face of an immature young man, a weak nose, a scrubby little moustache, a feeble chin. So for an instant we stood—he looking over his shoulder at me—and regarded one another. Then he seemed to remember his high calling. He turned round, drew himself up, projected his face, raised his arms, spread his hands in approved ghost fashion—came towards me. As he did so his little jaw dropped, and he emitted a faint, drawn-out 'Boo!' . . . No, it wasn't—not a bit dreadful. I was no

135

more frightened than if I'd been assailed by a frog. 'Boo!' I said. 'Nonsense. You don't belong to *this* place. What are you doing here?'

"I could see him wince. 'Boo-oo!' he said.

" 'Boo—be hanged! Are you a member?' I said; and just to show I didn't care a pin for him I stepped through a corner of him and made to light my candle. 'Are you a member?' I repeated, looking at him sideways.

"He moved a little so as to stand clear of me, and his bearing became crestfallen. 'No,' he said, in answer to the persistent interrogation of my eye; 'I'm not a member—I'm a ghost.'

" 'Well, that doesn't give you the run of the Mermaid Club. Is there anyone you want to see, or anything of that sort?' And doing it as steadily as possible for fear that he should mistake the carelessness of whisky for the distraction of fear, I got my candle alight. I turned on him, holding it. 'What are you doing here?' I said.

"He had dropped his hands and stopped his booing, and there he stood, abashed and awkward, the ghost of a weak, silly, aimless young man. 'I'm haunting,' he said.

" 'You haven't any business to,' I said in a quiet voice.

" 'I'm a ghost,' he said, as if in defence.

" 'That may be, but you haven't any business to haunt here. This is a respectable private club; people often stop here with nursemaids and children, and, going about in the careless way you do, some poor little mite could easily come upon you, and be scared out of her wits. I supposed you didn't think of that?'

" 'No, sir,' he said, 'I didn't.'

" 'You should have done. You haven't any claim on the place, have you? Weren't murdered here, or anything of that sort?'

" 'None, sir; but I thought as it was old and oak panelled—'

" 'That's no excuse.' I regarded him firmly. 'Your coming

here is a mistake,' I said, in a tone of friendly superiority. I feigned to see if I had my matches, and then looked up at him frankly. 'If I were you I wouldn't wait for cock-crow—I'd vanish right away.'

"He looked embarrassed. 'The fact *is*, sir—' he began.

" 'I'd vanish,' I said, driving it home.

" 'The fact is, sir, that—somehow—I can't.'

" 'You *can't*?'

" 'No, sir. There's something I've forgotten. I've been hanging about here since midnight last night, hiding in the cupboards of the empty bedrooms and things like that. I'm flurried. I've never come haunting before, and it seems to put me out.'

" 'Put you out?'

" 'Yes, sir. I've tried to do it several times, and it doesn't come off. There's some little thing has slipped me, and I can't get back.'

"That, you know, rather bowled me over. He looked at me in such an abject way that for the life of me I couldn't keep up quite the high hectoring vein I had adopted. 'That's queer,' I said, and as I spoke I fancied I heard someone moving about down below. 'Come into my room and tell me more about it,' I said. 'I didn't, of course, understand this,' and I tried to take him by the arm. But, of course, you might as well have tried to take hold of a puff of smoke! I had forgotten my number, I think; anyhow, I remember going into several bedrooms—it was lucky I was the only soul in that wing—until I saw my traps. 'Here we are,' I said, and sat down in the arm-chair; 'sit down and tell me all about it. It seems to me you have got yourself into a jolly awkward position, old chap.'

"Well, he said he wouldn't sit down; he'd prefer to flit up and down the room if it was all the same to me. And so he did, and in

137

a little while we were deep in a long and serious talk. And presently, you know, I began to realize just a little what a thundering rum and weird business it was that I was in. There he was semi-transparent—the proper conventional phantom, and noiseless except for his ghost of a voice—flitting to and fro in that nice, clean, chintz-hung old bedroom. You could see the gleam of the copper candlesticks through him, and the lights on the brass fender, and the corners of the framed engravings on the wall, and there he was telling me all about this wretched little life of his that had recently ended on earth. He hadn't a particularly honest face, you know, but being transparent, of course, he couldn't avoid telling the truth."

"Eh?" said Wish, suddenly sitting up in his chair.

"What?" said Clayton.

"Being transparent—couldn't avoid telling the truth—I don't see it," said Wish.

"*I* don't see it," said Clayton, with inimitable assurance. "But it *is* so, I can assure you nevertheless. I don't believe he got once a nail's breadth off the Bible truth. He told me how he had been killed—he went down into a London basement with a candle to look for a leakage of gas—and described himself as a senior English master in a London private school when that release occurred."

"Poor wretch!" said I.

"That's what *I* thought, and the more he talked the more I thought it. There he was, purposeless in life and purposeless out of it. He talked of his father and mother and his schoolmaster, and all who had ever been anything to him in the world, meanly. He had been too sensitive, too nervous; none of them had ever valued him properly or understood him, he said. He had never had a real friend in the world, I think; he had never had a success. He had shirked games and failed

138

examinations. 'It's like that with some people,' he said; 'whenever I got into the examination-room or anywhere everything seemed to go.' Engaged to be married, of course—to another over-sensitive person, I suppose—when the indiscretion with the gas escape ended his affairs. 'And where are you now?' I asked. 'Not in——?'

"He wasn't clear on that point at all. The impression he gave me was of a sort of vague, intermediate state, a special reserve for souls too non-existent for anything so positive as either sin or virtue. *I* don't know. He was much too egotistical and unobservant to give me any clear idea of the kind of place, kind of country, there is on the Other Side of Things. Wherever he was, he seems to have fallen in with a set of kindred spirits: ghosts of weak Cockney young men, who were on a footing of Christian names, and among these there was certainly a lot of talk about 'going haunting' and things like that. Yes—going haunting! They seemed to think 'haunting' a tremendous adventure, and most of them funked it all the time. And, so primed, you know, he had come."

"But really!" said Wish to the fire.

"These are the impressions he gave me, anyhow," said Clayton, modestly. "I may, of course, have been in a rather uncritical state, but that was the sort of background he gave to himself. He kept flitting up and down, with his thin voice going—talking, talking about his wretched self, and never a word of clear, firm statement from first to last. He was thinner and sillier and more pointless than if he had been real and alive. Only then, you know, he would not have been in my bedroom here—if he *had* been alive. I should have kicked him out."

"Of course," said Evans, "there *are* poor mortals like that."

"And there's just as much chance of their having ghosts as the rest of us," I admitted.

"What gave a sort of point to him, you know, was the fact that he did seem within limits to have found himself out. The mess he had made of haunting had depressed him terribly. He had been told it would be a 'lark': he had come expecting it to be a 'lark', and here it was nothing but another failure added to his record! He proclaimed himself an utter out-and-out failure. He said, and I can quite believe it, that he had never tried to do anything all his life that he hadn't made a perfect mess of—and through all the wastes of eternity he never would. If he had had sympathy, perhaps——He paused at that, and stood regarding me. He remarked that, strange as it might seem to me, nobody, not anyone, ever, had given him the amount of sympathy I was doing now. I could see what he wanted straight away, and I determined to head him off at once. I may be a brute, you know, but being the Only Real Friend, the recipient of the confidences of one of these egotistical weaklings, ghost or body, is beyond my physical endurance. I got up briskly. 'Don't you brood on these things too much,' I said. 'The thing you've got to do is to get out of this—get out of this sharp. You pull yourself together and *try*.' 'I can't,' he said. 'You try,' I said, and try he did."

"Try!" said Sanderson. "*How?*"

"Passes," said Clayton.

"Passes?"

"Complicated series of gestures and passes with the hands. That's how he had come in, and that's how he had to get out again. Lord! what a business I had!"

"But how could *any* series of passes——" I began.

"My dear man," said Clayton, turning on me and putting a great emphasis on certain words, "you want *everything* clear. I don't know *how*. All I know is that you *do*—that *he* did, anyhow, at least. After a fearful time, you know, he got his passes right and suddenly disappeared."

141

"Did you," said Sanderson slowly, "observe the passes?"

"Yes," said Clayton, and seemed to think. "It was tremendously queer," he said. "There we were, I and this thin vague ghost, in that silent room, in this silent, empty inn, in this silent little Friday-night town. Not a sound except our voices and a faint panting he made when he swung. There was the bedroom candle, and one candle on the dressing-table alight, that was all—sometimes one or other would flare up into a tall, lean, astonished flame for a space. And queer things happened. 'I can't,' he said; 'I shall never——!' And suddenly he sat down on a little chair at the foot of the bed and began to sob and sob. Lord! what a harrowing, whimpering thing he seemed!

" 'You pull yourself together,' I said, and tried to pat him on the back, and . . . my confounded hand went through him! By that time, you know, I wasn't nearly so—massive as I had been on the landing. I got the queerness of it full. I remember snatching back my hand out of him, as it were, with a little thrill, and walking over to the dressing-table. 'You pull yourself together', I said to him, 'and try.' And in order to encourage and help him I began to try as well."

"What!" said Sanderson, "the passes?"

"Yes, the passes."

"But——" I said, moved by an idea that eluded me for a space.

"This is interesting," said Sanderson, with his finger in his pipe-bowl. "You mean to say this ghost of yours gave away——"

"Did his level best to give away the whole confounded barrier? Yes."

"He didn't," said Wish; "he couldn't. Or you'd have gone there too."

"That's precisely it," I said, finding my elusive idea put into

142

words for me.

"That *is* precisely it," said Clayton, with thoughtful eyes upon the fire.

For just a little while there was silence.

"And at last he did it?" said Sanderson.

"At last he did it. I had to keep him up to it hard, but he did it at last—rather suddenly. He despaired, we had a scene, and then he got up abruptly and asked me to go through the whole performance, slowly, so that he might see. 'I believe', he said, 'if I could see I should spot what was wrong at once.' And he did. '*I* know,' he said. 'What do you know?' said I. '*I* know,' he repeated. Then he said peevishly, 'I can't do it, if you look at me—I really *can't*; it's been that, partly, all along. I'm such a nervous fellow that you put me out.' Well, we had a bit of an argument. Naturally I wanted to see; but he was as obstinate as a mule, and suddenly I had come over as tired as a dog—he tired me out. 'All right,' I said, '*I* won't look at you,' and turned towards the mirror, on the wardrobe, by the bed.

"He started off very fast. I tried to follow him by looking in the looking-glass, to see just what it was had hung fire. Round went his arms and his hands, so, and so, and so, and then with a rush came to the last gesture of all—you stand erect and open out your arms—and so, don't you know, he stood. And then he didn't! He didn't! He wasn't! I wheeled round from the looking-glass to him. There was nothing! I was alone with the flaring candles and a staggering mind. What had happened? Had anything happened? Had I been dreaming? . . . And then, with an absurd note of finality about it, the clock upon the landing discovered the moment was ripe for striking *one*. So!—Ping! And I was as grave and sober as a judge. Feeling queer, you know—confoundedly *queer*! Queer! Good Lord!"

He regarded his cigar-ash for a moment. "That's all that

143

happened," he said.

"And then you went to bed?" asked Evans.

"What else was there to do?"

I looked Wish in the eye. We wanted to scoff, and there was something, something perhaps in Clayton's voice and manner, that hampered our desire.

"And about these passes?" said Sanderson.

"I believe I could do them now."

"Oh!" said Sanderson, and produced a penknife and set himself to grub the dottle out of the bowl of his clay.

"Why don't you do them now?" said Sanderson, shutting his penknife with a click.

"That's what I'm going to do," said Clayton.

"They won't work," said Evans.

"If they do——" I suggested.

"You know, I'd rather you didn't," said Wish, stretching out his legs.

"Why?" asked Evans.

"I'd rather he didn't," said Wish.

"But he hasn't got 'em right," said Sanderson, plugging too much tobacco into his pipe.

"All the same, I'd rather he didn't," said Wish.

We argued with Wish. He said that for Clayton to go through those gestures was like mocking a serious matter. "But you don't believe——?" I said. Wish glanced at Clayton, who was staring into the fire, weighing something in his mind. "I do—more than half, anyhow, I do," said Wish.

"Clayton," said I, "you're too good a liar for us. Most of it was all right. But that disappearance . . . happened to be convincing. Tell us, it's a tale of cock and bull."

He stood up without heeding me, took the middle of the hearthrug, and faced me. For a moment he regarded his feet thoughtfully, and then for all the rest of the time his eyes were on the opposite wall, with an intent expression. He raised his two hands slowly to the level of his eyes and so began. . . .

Now, Sanderson is a Freemason, a member of the lodge of the Four Kings, which devotes itself so ably to the study and elucidation of all the mysteries of Masonry past and present, and among the students of this lodge Sanderson is by no means the least. He followed Clayton's motions with a singular interest in his reddish eye. "That's not bad," he said, when it was done. "You really do, you know, put things together, Clayton, in a most amazing fashion. But there's one little detail out."

"I know," said Clayton. "I believe I could tell you which."

"Well?"

"This," said Clayton, and did a queer little twist and writhing and thrust of the hands.

"Yes."

"That, you know, was what *he* couldn't get right," said Clayton. "But how do *you*——?"

"Most of this business, and particularly how you invented it, I don't understand at all," said Sanderson, "but just that phase—I do." He reflected. "These happen to be a series of gestures—connected with a certain branch of esoteric Masonry—— Probably you know. Or else——*How?*" He reflected still further. "I do not see I can do any harm in telling you just the proper twist. After all, if you know, you know; if you don't, you don't."

"I know nothing," said Clayton, "except what the poor devil let out last night."

"Well, anyhow," said Sanderson, and placed his churchwarden very carefully upon the shelf over the fireplace. Then very rapidly he gesticulated with his hands.

145

"So?" said Clayton, repeating.

"So," said Sanderson, and took his pipe in hand again.

"Ah, *now*", said Clayton, "I can do the whole thing—right."

He stood up before the waning fire and smiled at us all. But I think there was just a little hesitation in his smile. "If I begin——" he said.

"I wouldn't begin," said Wish.

"It's all right!" said Evans. "Matter is indestructible. You don't think any jiggery-pokery of this sort is going to snatch Clayton into the world of shades. Not it! You may try, Clayton, so far as I'm concerned, until your arms drop off at the wrists."

"I don't believe that," said Wish, and stood up and put his arm on Clayton's shoulder. "You've made me half believe in that story somehow, and I don't want to see the thing done."

"Goodness!" said I, "here's Wish frightened!"

"I am," said Wish, with real or admirably feigned intensity. "I believe that if he goes through these motions right he'll *go*."

"He'll not do anything of the sort!" I cried. "There's only one way out of this world for men, and Clayton is thirty years from that. Besides. . . . And such a ghost! Do you think——?"

Wish interrupted me by moving. He walked out from among our chairs and stopped beside the table and stood there. "Clayton," he said, "you're a fool."

Clayton, with a humorous light in his eyes, smiled back at him. "Wish", he said, "is right, and all you others are wrong. I shall go. I shall get to the end of these passes, and as the last swish whistles through the air, Presto!—this hearthrug will be vacant, the room will be blank amazement, and a respectably-dressed gentleman of fifteen stone will plump into the world of shades. I'm certain. So will you be. I decline to argue further. Let the thing be tried."

"*No*," said Wish, and made a step and ceased, and Clayton

raised his hands once more to repeat the spirit's passing.

By that time, you know, we were all in a state of tension—largely because of the behaviour of Wish. We sat all of us with our eyes on Clayton—I, at least, with a sort of tight, stiff feeling about me as though from the back of my skull to the middle of my thighs my body had been changed to steel. And there, with a gravity that was imperturbably serene, Clayton bowed and swayed and waved his hands and arms before us. As he drew towards the end one piled up, one tingled in one's teeth. The last gesture, I have said, was to swing the arms out wide open, with the face held up. And when, at last, he swung out to this closing gesture I ceased even to breathe. It was ridiculous, of course, but you know that ghost-story feeling. It was after dinner, in a queer, old, shadowy house. Would he, after all——?

There he stood for one stupendous moment, with his arms open and his upturned face, assured and bright, in the glare of the hanging lamp. We hung through that moment as if it were an age, and then came from all of us something that was half a sigh of infinite relief and half a reassuring "*No!*" For visibly—he wasn't going. It was all nonsense. He had told an idle story, and carried it almost to conviction, that was all! . . . And then in that moment the face of Clayton changed.

It changed. It changed as a lit house changes when its lights are suddenly extinguished. His eyes were suddenly eyes that were fixed, his smile was frozen on his lips, and he stood there still. He stood there, very gently swaying.

That moment, too, was an age. And then, you know, chairs were scraping, things were falling, and we were all moving. His knees seemed to give, and he fell forward, and Evans rose and caught him in his arms. . . .

It stunned us all. For a minute I suppose no one said a

coherent thing. We believed it, yet could not believe it. . . . I came out of a muddled stupefaction to find myself kneeling beside him, and his vest and shirt were torn open, and Sanderson's hand lay on his heart. . . .

Well—the simple fact before us could very well wait our convenience; there was no hurry for us to comprehend. It lay there for an hour; it lies athwart my memory, black and amazing still, to this day. Clayton had, indeed, passed into the world that lies so near to and so far from our own, and he had gone thither by the only road that mortal man may take. But whether he did indeed pass there by that poor ghost's incantation, or whether he was stricken suddenly by apoplexy in the midst of an idle tale—as the coroner's jury would have us believe—is no matter for my judging; it is just one of those inexplicable riddles that must remain unsolved until the final solution of all things shall come. All I certainly know is that, in the very moment, in the very instant, of concluding those passes, he changed, and staggered, and fell down before us—dead!

It

Norman Mailer's only ghost story (written in his teens) :

We were going through the barbed-wire,
when a machine gun started. I kept
walking until I saw my head lying on
the ground.

"My God, I'm dead," my head said.

And my body fell over.

Invitation to a Ghost

GEOFFREY PALMER and NOEL LLOYD

In which Ivan and Alexei, friends from childhood, pledge that whoever marries first will invite the other to his wedding, alive or dead . . . As it happens, Alexei dies young of a mysterious disease. On his wedding day Ivan goes to the graveyard to invite Alexei . . .

I VAN and Alexei had grown up together in the same village in Russia. They had played together as small children, gone to school together, and when they became young men they always went together to the *besyedas*, the evening gatherings where young people met to talk and sing and dance.

The two friends were also good-natured rivals. Sometimes Ivan would be the first to do a thing; at other times Alexei would score over his friend, but in the long run they were evenly matched in their accomplishments.

One day Ivan and Alexei were talking about their future, and the subject of marriage was naturally mentioned. They knew that they would not be able to see as much of each other when each of them had a wife to keep, but they made a solemn pact that whichever married first would invite the other to the wedding. Then followed more friendly rivalry. Who would be the bridegroom and who would be the wedding guest?

"If I marry first," said Ivan, "I'll invite you to the wedding

150

whether you're alive or dead!"

"That goes for me too," said Alexei solemnly.

Some months passed, during which the young men worked and played together, and then Alexei was suddenly stricken by a mysterious disease, and died after several weeks of illness. Ivan was very sad at losing his friend, and for a time felt lost and lonely. He recovered his high spirits, however, when he fell in love with one of the village girls, and when she agreed to marry him he was overjoyed.

On the wedding day Ivan and his family set off in a horse-drawn carriage to fetch his bride-to-be. On the way they laughed and sang, but as the procession neared the graveyard where Alexei was buried Ivan fell silent, suddenly remembering the pact he had made with his friend all those months before.

"Stop the horses!" he cried suddenly. "I must go to Alexei's grave!"

The driver pulled on the reins and the carriage stopped. Ivan leaped to the ground. "What are you going to do?" his father asked.

"I'm going to invite Alexei to the wedding," Ivan called, making his way to the graveyard. "He was my best friend, and I want him to take part in the rejoicing."

"But he's dead!" Ivan's mother wailed. "How can he be a wedding guest?"

"We made a pact, and I'm going to keep it." Ivan refused to listen to his family's protests. "I shan't be long," they heard him say before he disappeared into the darkness of the graveyard. The tombstones soon hid him from view.

Ivan stood before Alexei's grave. "Dear friend," he said, "I hope you can hear me because I've brought you an invitation to my wedding. I haven't forgotten my promise, you see."

A bitter wind blew across the desolate graveyard. Alexei's grave slowly opened and from the black cavity arose the pale, wasted figure of the dead man. "Thank you, friend, for remembering our pact," it said in a low, toneless voice. "I shall be glad to come to your wedding, but first let us drink together to celebrate the happy occasion. Step down with me into my abode."

Ivan hesitated, reluctant to admit to himself that he was frightened. "I would come with you, Alexei, but the carriage is waiting for me on the road outside the graveyard. I told my parents to stay until I had summoned you."

"Come, Ivan," Alexei pleaded. "It need not take us long to drink a glass in memory of the happy times we used to have. The carriage can surely wait a minute or two."

Ivan decided that he could not disappoint the ghost of his friend. He squared his shoulders and jumped into the open grave. The dead man poured out a cup of wine and handed it to Ivan. He raised it ceremoniously and drank, not realizing that, being in the domain of the dead, he was also in the time of the dead, and as he drank, time went by. . . .

"Another cup of wine," said the ghost of Alexei. Ivan began to protest, but the ghost took his cup, filled it and pressed it back in his hand, and Ivan was forced to drink again. As he drank, time went by. . . .

"Now I must join my family," said Ivan, eager to be out of the dark cavern. But the ghost of Alexei restrained him.

"A third cup, I beg of you, and then go to your marriage. I shall not come with you—I do not think the other guests would welcome me. Drink this last cup in memory of our friendship, before we say farewell." The ghost poured wine into Ivan's cup, and as he drank, time went by. . . .

"Farewell, my friend!" The words came faintly as the ghost sank back into the grave and the lid of the coffin closed after him. Then there was silence.

With the wine singing in his head Ivan clambered out of the grave and looked about him. To his amazement the landscape seemed to have changed in the few minutes he had been drinking with his friend. The grave itself had disappeared under a tangle of weeds and overgrown bushes. The graveyard had changed into a stretch of wasteland. There was no sign of a road, and where the carriage had been waiting for him patches of tall nettles grew.

Ivan stared at the unfamiliar scene, panic gradually rising in him. The he began to run, back to the village he had set out from earlier in such high spirits. Surely he would find everything normal there! Surely he would find an explanation of this strange happening!

But more surprises awaited him in the village. It was nothing like the place in which he had been born and had grown up. The houses were built in a different style, the roads went in different directions. All the people were strangers. Instead of recognizing every single person, he could not see a single face he knew.

Only the church seemed familiar, though he could not remember it being so broken-down; it was almost a ruin. He could not trust himself to speak to any of the strange people walking about the streets. He would not have known what to say to them. But perhaps the priest could help him, and tell him what had happened to the world he had known. Father Vishnoff was old, and wise, and kind. He would make everything come right. . . .

But it was not Father Vishnoff who opened the door of the church to Ivan's frantic knocking. It was a younger man, with dark hair and a brisk, businesslike manner. "What can I do for

154

you, young man?" he said, looking at the wild-eyed Ivan cautiously.

Ivan's story came out jerkily. The priest listened, his expression unchanging. "What has happened?" Ivan finished, spreading out his hands imploringly. "You must help me—I'm so confused!"

The priest frowned and shook his head, thinking that this agitated young man was out of his mind. He uttered a few soothing words and prepared to step back into the church, closing the door behind him. But Ivan followed. He clutched the priest's arm, crying, "Please help me! Why has everything changed? Where am I? What has happened?"

The priest looked searchingly at him, then came to a decision. "Tell me your story again," he commanded, and led Ivan to a seat in the church.

When Ivan came to the end of the second telling the priest looked very thoughtful. Then he grunted, "Come with me." He took Ivan into a room full of dusty, leather-covered books, and pulled one of them down from a shelf. "These are the church records going back for many, many years," he said. "Sit down, and we will go through them."

For hours they read through books and documents, going backwards in time, searching for any mention of Ivan and Alexei and the village people that Ivan had spoken about. They grew tired and red-eyed. The room grew dim. At last the priest gasped and pointed a shaking finger at a yellowing page.

"Read!" he ordered.

Ivan focused his blurred gaze on the faded writing. Slowly, unbelievingly, he read the story of a bridegroom who had gone into the graveyard on his wedding day, had disappeared and had never been seen or heard of since. His family had waited for him to return, then had hunted for him high and low. When they had been unable to find any trace of him they decided that he had been carried off by demons. The waiting bride-to-be had collapsed with shock. She had been ill for a long time afterwards, then had recovered and eventually married another man. . . .

Ivan turned an incredulous face to the priest. "But how can that be?" he asked. "Here I am now—ready to go with my family and be married at once."

The priest looked at him sadly. "The date, my son, did you not notice the date? The account you have just read was written three hundred years ago. You drank with the ghost of your friend. You are now a ghost yourself. . . ."

An Apparition

KNUT HAMSUN

In which a young boy, playing in a churchyard, finds a tooth and takes it home in his pocket. That night a strange apparition comes to collect it . . .

SEVERAL years of my childhood were spent with my uncle at the vicarage in Norland. It was a hard time for me—much work, much thrashing, and seldom if ever a time for play and amusement. My uncle was so strict with me that little by little it became my only joy to slip away and be alone. If I occasionally had a free hour, I slipped into the woods, or went up to the churchyard, and wandered among the graves and the crosses, dreaming, thinking, and talking aloud to myself.

The vicarage had an exceptionally beautiful site along the Glimma, a river, wide, and boulder strewn. Day and night its voice sounded. At one time of the day Glimma moved south at another time north, according to the ebb and flow of the tide; but unceasingly its eternal song murmured, and its waters moved with the same haste summer or winter, whatever path it took.

The church, and the churchyard were on a hill. The building was an old frame chapel, built in the form of a cross; the churchyard was without care of any sort, and always without flowers on the graves; but over near the stone wall were wont to grow the most luscious raspberries, a large and juicy fruit that drew nourishment from the rich mould below. I knew every grave and every inscription, and many a cross that I saw set up new, in time began to lean, and at last, on a stormy night, toppled over.

But if there were no flowers on the graves, there was a luxuriant growth of grass over the entire churchyard. It was so tall and so coarse that I often sat there listening to the wind that soughed through the very hard growth that reached to my waist. Often in the midst of this sighing, the weathercock on the steeple of the church swung about, and the rasp of the rusty iron sounded complainingly over the whole vicarage plot. It was as if this bit of iron were cutting its teeth against another piece of iron.

When the sexton was working, I often talked to him. He was a serious fellow who seldom smiled, but he was very friendly to me, and as he stood casting up the earth from the grave he was digging, he would often warn me to be gone, for now he had on his spade a large thigh bone, or a grinning skull.

I often found on the graves bits of bones that I had always put back into the earth again as the sexton had taught me. I was so used to this that I felt no abhorrence in coming upon these human relics. Under one end of the church was a burial cellar where masses of bones lay scattered, and in this vault I sat many an hour, hammering on something, or making varied designs on the floor with the mouldering bones.

But one day I found a tooth in the churchyard. It was a front tooth, strong, and of a brilliant white. Without giving myself any reason for it, I put the tooth into my pocket. I would use it for something, file it into some sort of design, and inlay it into

158

one of the many wonderful things I made of wood. I took the tooth home with me.

It was autumn, and dusk came early. I had one and another thing to do, and probably two hours passed before I went into the kitchen to work on the tooth. In the meantime the moon—half full—had arisen.

There was no light in the kitchen, and I was quite alone. I did not dare to light the lamps, because the beetles would come, but I could manage with the light from the vent in the stove, when I got a good fire going. So I went into the shed for wood.

The shed was dark. While I was fumbling for the wood, I felt a light blow, as from a single finger, on my head.

I turned about hastily, but saw no one. I thrashed about me with my arms, but felt no one. I called, asking if anyone were there, but I received no answer.

I was bareheaded. I reached up to the spot on my head where I had been struck, and against my hand I felt something so icy cold that I immediately relaxed my hold. "How strange that is!" I thought. I reached again toward my hair—the chill had disappeared. I thought, "What can it be that has fallen from the roof and struck my head?"

I took an armful of wood and went into the kitchen, fired the stove, and waited until the light came from the vent. Then I took out the tooth and the file.

There was the sound of knocking on the window!

I looked up. Beyond the window, with his face pressed close to the pane, stood a man. He was a stranger to me. I did not know him although I knew everyone in the parish. He had a full, red beard and a red scarf about his throat, and a sou'wester on his head. What I did not think of then, but what occurred to me later was this: How could this be? How could his head appear to me so clearly in the dark, even from a part of the house

where not even the half moon was shining? I saw the face with an appalling clearness. It was pale, almost white, and its eyes were staring right at me.

A minute went by. Then the man began to smile. It was no audible, stirring laughter, but the mouth opened wide, and the eyes continued to stare as before, but the man smiled.

I dropped what I had in my hands, and trembled from head to foot. In the ugly gap of the leering face outside the window pane I suddenly saw a yawning space in the row of teeth. A tooth was missing!

I sat and stared before me in agony. Another minute went by. The face began to change colour. It became deeply green, then deeply red, but the smile remained fixed. I was not unconscious; I could note everything about me. The fire burned quite clearly in the vent of the stove, and cast a pale glow even to the stairway at the opposite wall. I could also hear within the maid's room on the other side of the wall, a clock ticking. I saw everything so clearly that I even noticed that the sou'wester that the man outside the window wore was a rusty black in the crown but had a green brim.

Then the man lowered his head down along the pane, very slowly, farther and farther down, and at last he was below the window. It was as if he glided into the ground. I could no longer see him.

My fright was terrible. I began to shiver. I slipped to the floor to find the tooth, but at the same time I did not dare to take my eyes from the window, lest the face should again appear.

When I had found the tooth, I would have taken it back at once to the churchyard but I didn't dare to. I continued to sit alone; I could not move. I heard steps out in the yard, and saw one of the maidservants come clattering along in her wooden shoes; but I did not dare to call to her, and the steps went past.

An eternity passed; the fire began to burn out in the stove; no rescue appeared for me.

Then I clenched my teeth together, and I arose. I opened the door, and moved backwards, out of the scullery, constantly gazing toward the window where the man had stood. When I came out into the yard, I took to my heels to the stable where I would find one of the stable boys to go with me to the churchyard.

But the boys were not in the stable.

In the meantime I had become bolder, out under the open sky, and I determined to go alone to the churchyard; moreover, I wished to escape confiding in someone, and perhaps, later find myself in my uncle's clutches, and forced to tell him the story. So I went alone up over the hill, carrying the tooth in my pocket handkerchief.

Near the gate of the churchyard I paused; my courage refused to stay with me any longer. I heard the eternal sound of the river, but otherwise all was silent. There was no door in the churchyard portal, only an archway to pass through; I stationed myself anxiously on one side of this archway and thrust my head carefully into its aperture to see if I should advance.

Then I sank on my knees in the pathway! A short distance beyond the gate, between the graves, stood my man with the seaman's hat. He had the same white face, and as he turned it toward me he beckoned me forward, up into the churchyard.

I interpreted this as a command, but I did not dare to go. I lay there a long time and looked at the man; I prayed to him, but he stood there, silent.

Then something happened that gave me a little courage again. I heard one of the stable boys moving about some task down near the barnyard. This sign of life about me caused me to rise. The man began, very slowly, to move off; he did not walk, but glided over the graves, beckoning me steadily forward. I stepped inside the gate; the man beckoned me nearer. I took a few steps, and stood still, I could go no farther. With a trembling hand I took the white tooth from my handkerchief and threw it with all my might into the churchyard. At that instant, the iron cock on the church steeple swung around and its cutting shriek penetrated my bone and marrow. I rushed through the gate and down over the slope, homeward. When I came into the scullery, they saw that my face was white as snow.

Many years have passed since then, but I recollect it all. I still see myself kneeling by the gate of the churchyard, and I see the man with the red beard. I cannot even approximate his age. He might have been twenty years, or he might have been forty. As it was not to be the last time I saw him, I thought later about this, but I do not know even now what I should say about his age.

The man came back many an evening, many a night. He appeared, smiled with the broad grin that showed his missing tooth, and vanished.

The snow came, and I could no longer go up to the churchyard to put the tooth into the earth. And the man continued to come through the entire winter, but at greater intervals. My harrowing fear disappeared, but he made my days very unhappy, beyond measure unhappy. Many times in those days I derived a little joy from thinking that I could end my torture by throwing myself into the Glimma at flood tide.

Then spring came, and the man vanished altogether.

Altogether? No, not wholly, but for the entire summer. The next winter he appeared again. He came only once, then remained away for a long time. Three years after my first meeting with him I left Norland and was gone for a year. When I came back I was confirmed, and I seemed to myself a grown person. I no longer resided with my uncle at the vicarage but at home with my father and mother.

One afternoon in the fall when I had lain down to sleep, a cold hand was laid on my forehead. I opened my eyes, and saw the man before me seated in a chair by the bed. I was not sleeping alone in the room, but with two of my brothers. I awoke neither of them. When I felt the cold pressure on my forehead, I raised my hands and said, "Go away."

My brothers called from their beds and asked to whom I spoke.

When the man had sat still for a short time, he began to rock back and forth with his body. While doing this he began to rise, until at last he swayed almost up to the ceiling. When it appeared that he could go no farther, he arose fully, and glided with lifeless steps over the floor away from my bed to the stove, where he vanished.

He had never been so near to me as then. I had looked directly into his face. His glance was vacant, yet sly; he looked at me, but as if past me, right through me, far off to another world. I noticed that he had grey eyes. He did not move his features; he did not smile. When I shoved his hand from my forehead and said, "Go away," he drew his hand away slowly. During all the time he sat by my bed, he did not blink his eyes.

A few months later when winter had come and I had left home again, I lived for a time at the house of a merchant, Mr. W., whom I helped in the shop and in the office. Here I was to meet my man for the last time.

I went up to my room one evening, lighted the lamp, and

164

undressed. As usual, I was going to set my shoes out for the boy to clean and taking them in my hand, I opened the door.

There he stood in the corridor, directly before me—that red-bearded man!

I knew that there were persons in the adjoining rooms, so I wasn't afraid. I mumbled, audibly, "Are *you* here again?" A moment later the man opened his large mouth, and began to smile. This no longer made any agonizing impression on me, but this time I became more attentive. The missing tooth had come back to its place!

Perhaps someone had put it down into the ground. Or perhaps through the years it had managed to crumble, to disintegrate, to become one with the dust from which it had become separated. God only knows!

The man closed his mouth, but I still stood in the doorway; he turned around and went down the stairway at the foot of which he vanished.

I have never seen him again, and many years have passed since then. . . .

This man, the red-bearded messenger from the land of death, has, with the inexpressible horror that he brought into my childhood, done me much harm. I have had more than one vision since then, more than one strange encounter with the Inexplicable, but nothing has impressed me so strongly as this.

Yet perhaps he has not done me only harm. This has often occurred to me. I could believe that he was one of the first reasons why I learned to clench my teeth and to harden myself. In later life I have certainly had need for that.

The Apple Tree

ELIZABETH BOWEN

*In which the members of a week-end house party are rather
unnerved by the strange behaviour of their host's young wife.*

"FRIGHTENED!" exclaimed Lancelot. "Of her? Oh,
nonsense—surely? She's an absolute child."

"But *that's* what I mean," said Mrs. Bettersley, glancing
queerly sideways at him over the collar of her fur coat. He still
did not know what she meant, and did not think she knew
either.

In a rather nerve-racking combination of wind and moonlight Simon Wing's week-end party picked its way back to his
house, by twos and threes, up a cinder-path from the village.
Simon, who entered with gusto into his new role of squire, had
insisted that they should attend the Saturday concert in the
village memorial hall, a raftered, charmless and icy building
endowed by himself and only recently opened. Here, with
numbing feet and creeping spines, they had occupied seven
front seats, under a thin but constant spate of recitation,
pianoforte duet and song, while upon them from all quarters
draughts directed themselves like arrows. To restore circulation they had applauded vigorously, too often precipitating an
encore. Simon, satisfied with his friends, with his evening,

leaned forward to beam down the row. He said this would please the village. Lancelot communicated to Mrs. Bettersley a suspicion; this was why Simon had asked them down.

"So I'm afraid," she replied, "and for church tomorrow."

All the same, it had warmed them all to see Simon happy. Mounting the platform to propose a vote of thanks to the Vicar, the great ruddy man had positively expanded; glowed; a till now too palpable cloud rolled away from him. It was this recognition by his old friends of the old Simon—a recognition so instantaneous, poignant and cheerful that it was like a handshake, a first greeting—that now sent the party so cheerfully home in its twos and threes, their host ever boisterously ahead. At the tail, lagging, Lancelot and Mrs. Bettersley fell into a discussion of Simon—his marriage, his ménage, his whole aspect marked by entire unrestraint; as though between these two also some shadow had dissipated. They were old friendly enemies.

"But a child——" resumed Lancelot.

"Naturally I didn't mean to suggest that she was a werewolf!"

"You think she *is* what's the matter?"

"Obviously there's nothing funny about the house."

Obviously there was nothing funny about the house. Under the eerie cold sky, pale but not bright with moonlight, among bare, wind-shaken trees, the house's bulk loomed, honourably substantial. Lit-up windows sustained the party with promise of indoor comfort: firelight on decanters, room after room heavy-curtained; Simon's feeling for home made concrete (at last, after wandering years) in deep leather chairs, padded fenders and sectional bookcases, "domes of silence" on yielding carpets; and unaspiring, comfortable sobriety.

"She does seem to me only half there," confessed Lancelot;

167

"not, of course, I mean, mentally, but——"

"She had that frightful time—don't you know? *Don't* you know?" Mrs. Bettersley brightened, approaching her lips to his ear in the half moonlight. "She was at that school—don't you remember? After all *that*, the school broke up, you know. She was sent straight abroad—she'd have been twelve at the time I dare say; in a pretty state, I've no doubt, poor child!—to an aunt and uncle at Cannes. Her only relations; they lived out there in a villa, never came home—she stayed abroad with them. It was then Simon met her; then this."

"School?" said Lancelot, stuttering with excitement. "What—were they ill-treated?"

"Heavens, not that!" exclaimed Mrs. Bettersley. "Worse——"

But just at this point—it was unbearable—they saw the party pull up and contract ahead. Simon was waiting to shepherd them through the gate, to lock the gate after them.

"I hope," he said, beaming as they came up, "you weren't too bored."

They could not fail to respond.

"It's been a marvellous evening," said Mrs. Bettersley; Lancelot adding, "What wonderful talent you've got round here!"

"I don't think we're bad for a village," said Simon modestly, clicking the gate to. "The choral society are as keen as mustard. And I always think that young Dickinson ought to go on the stage. I'd pay to see him anywhere."

"Oh, so would I," agreed Lancelot cordially. "It's too sad," he added, "your wife having missed all this."

Simon's manner contracted. "She went to the dress rehearsal," he said quickly.

"Doesn't she act herself?"

168

"I can't get her to try.... Well, here we are; here we are!" Simon shouted, stamping across the terrace.

Young Mrs. Wing had been excused the concert. She had a slight chill, she feared. If she ever did cast any light on village society it was tonight withheld. No doubt Simon was disappointed. His friends, filing after him through the french window into the library, all hoped that by now—it was half-past ten—young Mrs. Simon might have taken her chill to bed.

But from the hearth her flat little voice said, "Hullo!" There she still stood, looking towards the window, watching their entrance as she watched their exit. Her long, silver sheath of a dress made her almost grown up. So they all prepared with philosophy to be nice to young Mrs. Wing. They all felt this week-end party, this incursion of old friends all knit up with each other, so knit up round Simon, might well be trying for young Mrs. Wing. In the nature even, possibly, of an ordeal. She was barely nineteen, and could not, to meet them, be expected to put up anything of "a manner". She had them, however, at a slight disadvantage, for Simon's marriage had been a shock for his friends. He had been known for years as a likely marrying man; so much so that his celibacy appeared an accident, but his choice of a wife—this mannerless, sexless child, the dim something between a mouse and an Undine, this wraith not considerable as a mother of sons, this cold little shadow across a hearth—had considerably surprised them. By her very passivity she attacked them when they were least prepared.

Mrs. Wing, at a glance from her husband, raised a silver lid from some sandwiches with a gesture of invitation. Mrs. Bettersley, whose appetite was frankly wolfish, took two, and slipping out inch by inch from her fur coat, lined up beside her little hostess in the firelight, solid and brilliant. The others

169

divided arm-chairs in the circle of warmth.

"Did you have a nice concert?" said Mrs. Wing politely. No-one could answer. "It went off well on the whole," said Simon gently, as though breaking sorrowful news to her.

Lancelot could not sleep. The very comfort of the bed, the too exquisite sympathy with his body of springs and mattress, became oppressive. Wind had subsided, moonlight sketched a window upon his floor. The house was quiet, too quiet; with jealousy and nostalgia he pictured them all sleeping. Mrs. Wing's cheek would scarcely warm a pillow. In despair Lancelot switched the light on; the amiable furniture stared. He read one page of *Our Mutual Friend* with distaste, and decided to look downstairs for a detective story. He slept in a corridor branching off from the head of the main staircase.

Downstairs the hall was dark, rank with cooling cigar-smoke. A clock struck three; Lancelot violently started. A little moon came in through the skylight; the library door was closed; stepping quietly, Lancelot made his way to it. He opened the door, saw red embers, then knew in a second the library was not empty. All the same, in there in the dark they were not moving or speaking.

Embarrassment—had he surprised an intrigue?—and abrupt physical fear—were these burglars?—held Lancelot bound on the threshold. Certainly someone was not alone; in here, in spite of the dark, someone was watching someone. He did not know whether to speak. He felt committed by opening the door, and standing against the grey of the glass-roofed hall must be certainly visible.

Finally it was Simon's voice that said defensively: "Hullo!" Lancelot knew he must go away immediately. He had only one wish—to conceal his identity. But Simon, apparently, did not

170

trust one; moving bulkily, he came down the long room to the door, bumping, as though in a quite unfamiliar room, against the furniture, his arm out ahead, as though pushing aside or trying to part a curtain. He seemed to have no sense of distance; Lancelot ducked, but a great hand touched his face. The hand was ice-cold.

"Oh, you?" said Simon. From his voice, his breath, he had been drinking heavily. He must still be holding a glass in his other hand—Lancelot heard whisky slopping about as the glass shook.

"It's all right," said Lancelot; "I was just going up. Sorry," he added.

"You can't—come—in—here," said Simon obstinately.

"No, I say; I was just going up." Lancelot stopped; friendliness fought in him with an intense repulsion. Not that he minded—though this itself was odd; Simon hardly ever touched anything.

But the room was a trap, a cul-de-sac; Simon, his face less than a yard away, seemed to be speaking to him through bars. He was frightful in fear; a man with the humility of a beast; he gave off fear like some disagreeable animal smell, making Lancelot dislike and feel revolted by his own humanity, his own manhood, as though in too close proximity with someone alien.

"Go away," said Simon, pushing at him in the dark. Lancelot stepped back in alarm, a rug slipped under his foot, he staggered, grasping at the lintel of the door. His elbow knocked a switch; immediately the hall, with its four hanging lamps, sprang into brilliant illumination. One was staggered by this explosion of light; Lancelot put his hands over his eyes; when he took them away he could see Simon's face was clammy, mottled; here and there a bead of sweat trembled and ran down.

171

He was standing sideways, his shoulder against the door; past him a path of light ran into the library.

Mrs. Simon stood just out of the light, looking fixedly up and pointing at something above her head. Round her Lancelot distinguished the big chairs, the table with the decanters, and, faintly, the glazed bookcases. Her eyes, looking up, reflected the light but did not flicker, she did not stir. With an exclamation, a violent movement, Simon shut the library door. They both stood outside its white glossy panels. By contrast with what stood inside, staring there in the dark, Simon was once more human; unconsciously, as much to gain as to impart re-assurance, Lancelot put a hand on his arm.

Not looking at one another, they said nothing.

They were in no sense alone even here, for the slam of the door produced, in a moment or two, Mrs. Bettersley, who looked down at them from the gallery just overhead the zone of bright lights, her face sharpened and wolfish from vehement curiosity. Lancelot looked up; their eyes met.

"All right, only somebody sleep-walking," he called up softly.

"All right," she replied, withdrawing; but not, he guessed, to her room; rather to lean back in shadow against the wall of the gallery, impassive, watchful, arms folded over the breast of her dark silk kimono.

A moment later she still made no sign—he would have been glad of her presence. For the return to Simon of sensibility and intelligence, like circulation beginning again in a limb that had been tightly bound up, was too much for Simon. One side-glance that almost contained his horror, then—huge figure, crumpling, swaying, sagging—he fainted suddenly. Lancelot broke his fall a little and propped him, sitting, against the wall.

This left Lancelot much alone. He noted details; a dog-collar lying unstrapped, ash trodden into the rug, a girl's gloves—probably Mrs. Simon's—dropped crumpled into a big brass tray. Now drawn to the door—aware the whole time of his position's absurdity—he knelt, one ear to the keyhole. Silence. In there she must still stand in contemplation—horrified, horrifying—of something high up that from the not quite fixity of her gaze had seemed unfixed, pendant, perhaps swaying a little. Silence. Then—he pressed closer—a thud—thud—thud—three times, like apples falling.

This idea of apples entered his mind and remained, frightfully clear; an innocent pastoral image seen black through a dark transparency. This idea of fruit detaching itself and, from a leafy height, falling in the stale, shut-up room had the sharpness of an hallucination; he thought he was going mad.

"Come down," he called up to the gallery.

Mrs. Bettersley, with that expectant half-smile, appeared immediately, and came downstairs. She glanced at Simon's unconsciousness, for which she seemed to be grateful, then went to the library door. After a moment facing the panels, she tried the handle, cautiously turning it.

"*She's* in here," said Lancelot.

"Coming?" she asked.

He replied "No," very frankly and simply.

"Oh, well," she shrugged; "I'm a woman," and entered the library, pushing the door to behind her. He heard her moving among the furniture. "Now come," she said, "come, my dear. . . ." After a moment or two of complete silence and stillness: "Oh, my God, no—I can't!" she exclaimed. She came out again, very white. She was rubbing her hands together as though she had hurt them. "It's impossible," she repeated. "One can't get past . . . it's like an apple tree."

She knelt by Simon and began fumbling with his collar. Her

173

hands shook. Lancelot watched the access of womanly busyness.

The door opened again and young Mrs. Wing came out in her nightgown, hair hanging over her shoulders in two plaits, blinking under the strong light. Seeing them all she paused in natural confusion.

"I walk in my sleep," she murmured, blushed and slipped past upstairs without a glance at her husband, still in confusion, like any other young woman encountered by strangers in her nightgown, her appearance and disappearance the very picture of modest precipitancy.

Simon began to come to. Mrs. Bettersley also retreated. The fewest possible people ought, they felt, to be in on this.

Sunday morning was pale blue, mild and sunny. Mrs. Bettersley appeared punctually for breakfast, beaming, pink and impassible. Lancelot looked pale and puffy; Mrs. Simon did not appear. Simon came in like a tempered Boreas to greet the party, rubbing his hands. After breakfast they stepped out through the window to smoke on the terrace. Church, said Simon pressingly, would be at eleven.

Mrs. Bettersley revolted. She said she liked to write letters on a Sunday morning. The rest, with a glance of regret at the shining November garden, went off like lambs. When they had gone she slipped upstairs and tapped on Mrs. Simon's door.

The young woman was lying comfortably enough, with a fire burning, a mild novel open face down on the counterpane. This pretty bride's room, pink and white, frilled and rosy, now full of church bells and winter sunshine, had for Mrs. Bettersley, in all its appointments, an air of anxious imitation and approximation to some idea of the grown-up. Simon's bed was made and the room in order.

"You don't mind?" said Mrs. Bettersley, having sat down

174

firmly.

Mrs. Simon said nervously she was so pleased.

"All right this morning?"

"Just a little chill, I think."

"And no wonder! Do you often walk in your sleep?"

Mrs. Simon's small face tightened, hardened, went a shade whiter among the pillows. "I don't know," she said. Her manner became a positive invitation to Mrs. Bettersley to go away. Flattening among the bedclothes, she tried hard to obliterate herself.

Her visitor, who had not much time—for, the bells stopped, they would be back again in an hour—was quite merciless. "How old were you", she said, "when *that* happened?"

"Twelve—please don't——"

"You never told anyone?"

"No—please, Mrs. Bettersley—please, not now. I feel so ill."

"You're making Simon ill."

"Do you think I don't know?" the child exclaimed. "I thought he'd save me. I didn't think he'd ever be frightened. I didn't know any power could. . . . Indeed, indeed, Mrs. Bettersley, I had no idea. . . . I felt so safe with him. I thought this would go away. Now when it comes it is twice as horrible. Do you think it is killing him?"

"I shouldn't wonder," said Mrs. Bettersley.

"Oh, oh," moaned Mrs. Wing, and, with wrists crossed over her face, shook all over, sobbing so that the bedhead rattled against the wall. "He was so sorry for me," she moaned; "it was more than I could resist. He was so sorry for me. Wouldn't you feel Simon might save you?"

Mrs. Bettersley, moving to the edge of the bed, caught the girl's wrists and firmly, but not untenderly, forced them apart, disclosing the small convulsed face and fixed eyes. "We've got

175

three-quarters of an hour alone," she said. "You've got to tell me. Make it come into words. When it's once out it won't hurt—like a tooth, you know. Talk about it like anything. Talk to Simon. You never have, have you? You never do?"

Mrs. Bettersley felt quite a brute, she told Lancelot later. She had, naturally, in taking this hard line, something to go on. Seven years ago, newspapers had been full of the Crampton Park School tragedy; a little girl's suicide. There had been some remarkable headlines, some details, profuse speculation. Influence from some direction having been brought to bear, the affair disappeared from the papers abruptly. Some suggestion of things having been "hushed up" gave the affair, in talk, a fresh, cruel prominence; it became a topic. One hinted at all sorts of scandal. The school broke up, the staff disappeared, discredited; the fine house and grounds, in the West Country, were sold at a loss. One pupil, Myra Conway, felt the shock with surprising keenness. She nearly died of brain fever; collapsing the day after the suicide, she remained at death's door for weeks, alone with her nurses in the horrified house, Crampton Park. All the other children were hurried away. One heard afterwards that her health, her nerves, had been ruined. The other children presumably rallied; one heard no more of them. Myra Conway became Myra Wing. So much they all knew, even Simon.

Myra Wing now lay on her side in bed, in her pink bedroom, eyes shut, cheek pressed to the pillow as though she were sleeping, but with her body rigid; gripping with both hands Mrs. Bettersley's arm. She spoke slowly, choosing her words with diffidence as though hampered by trying to speak an unfamiliar language.

"I went there when I was ten. I don't think it can ever have

176

been a very good school. They called it a home school, I suppose, because most of us stayed for the holidays—we had no parents—and none of us was over fourteen. From being there so much we began to feel that this was the world. There was a very high wall round the garden. I don't think they were unkind to us, but everything seemed to go wrong. Doria and I were always in trouble. I suppose that was why we knew each other. There were about eighteen other girls, but none of them liked us. We used to feel we had some disease—so much so that we were sometimes ashamed to meet each other; sometimes we did not like to be together. I don't think we knew we were unhappy; we never spoke of that; we should have felt ashamed. We used to pretend we were all right; we got, in a way, to be quite proud of ourselves, of being different. I think, though, we made each other worse. In those days I was very ugly. Doria was as bad; she was very queer-looking; her eyes goggled, and she wore big round glasses. I suppose if we had had parents it would have been different. As it was, it was impossible to believe anyone could ever care for either of us. We did not even care for each other; we were just like two patients in hospital, shut away from the others because of having some frightful disease. But I suppose we depended on one another.

"The other children were mostly younger. The house was very large and dark-looking, but full of pictures to make it look homely. The grounds were very large, full of trees and laurels. When I was twelve I felt if this was the world I could not bear it. When I was twelve I got measles; another girl of my age got the measles too, and we were sent to a cottage to get well. She was very pretty and clever; we made friends; she told me she did not mind me, but she could not bear Doria. When we both got well and went back to the others, I loved her so much I felt I could not bear to part from her. She had a home of her own; she was

177

very happy and gay; to know her and hear about her life was like heaven. I took great trouble to please her; we went on being friends. The others began to like me; I ran away from Doria. Doria was left alone. She seemed to be all that was horrible in my life; from the moment we parted things began to go right with me. I laughed at her with the others.

"The only happy part of Doria's life and mine in the bad days were the games we played and the stories we told in a lonely part of the garden, a slope of lawn with one beautiful old apple tree. Sometimes we used to climb up in the branches. Nobody else ever came there, it was like something of our own; to be there made us feel happy and dignified.

"Doria was miserable when I left her. She never wept; she used to walk about by herself. It was as though everything I had got free of had fallen on her, too; she was left with my wretchedness. When I was with the others I used to see her, always alone, watching me. One afternoon she made me come with her to the apple tree; I was sorry for her and went; when we got there I could not bear it. I was so frightened of being lost again; I said terrible things to her. I wished she was dead. You see, there seemed to be no other world outside the school.

"She and I still slept in the same room, with two others. That night—there was some moon—I saw her get up. She tied the cord of her dressing-gown—it was very thick—round her waist tightly; she looked once at me, but I pretended to be asleep. She went out and did not come back. I lay—there was only a little moon—with a terrible feeling, like something tight round my throat. At last I went down to look for her. A glass door of the garden was open. I went out to look for her. She had hanged herself, you know, in the apple tree. When I first got there I saw nothing. I looked round and called her, and shook the branches, but only—it was September—two or three apples fell down.

178

The leaves kept brushing against my face. Then I saw her. Her feet were just over my head. I parted the branches to look—there was just enough moon—the leaves brushed my face. I crept back into bed and waited. No-one knew; no steps came. Next morning, of course, they did not tell us anything. They said she was ill. I pretended to know no better. I could not think of anything but the apple tree.

"While I was ill—I was very ill—I thought the leaves would choke me. Whenever I moved in bed an apple fell down. All the girls were taken away. When I got well, I found the house was empty. The first day I could, I crept out alone to look for the real apple tree. 'It is only a tree,' I thought; 'if I could see it, I should be quite well.' But the tree had been cut down. The place where it grew was filled with new turf. The nurse swore to me there had never been an apple tree there at all. She did not know—no one ever knew—I had been out that night and seen Doria.

"I expect you can guess the rest—you were there last night. You see, I am haunted. It does not matter where I am, or who I am with. Though I am married now, it is just the same. Every now and then—I don't know yet when or what brings it about—I wake to see Doria get up and tie the cord round her waist and go out. I have to go after her; there is always the apple tree. Its roots are in me. It takes all my strength, and now it's beginning to take Simon's.

"Those nights, no-one can bear to be with me. Everyone who has been with me knows, but no-one will speak of it. Only Simon tries to be there, those times—you saw, last night. It is impossible to be with me; I make rooms impossible. I am not like a house that can be burnt, you see, or pulled down. You know how it is—I heard you in there last night, trying to come to me——"

180

"I won't fail again: I've never been more ashamed," said Mrs. Bettersley.

"If I stay up here the tree grows in the room; I feel it will choke Simon. If I go out, I find it darker than all the others against the sky. . . . This morning I have been trying to make up my mind; I must go; I must leave Simon. I see quite well this is destroying him. Seeing him with you all makes me see how he used to be, how he might have been. You see, it's hard to go. He's my life. Between all this . . . we're so happy. But make me do this, Mrs. Bettersley!"

"I'll make you do one thing. Come away with me—perhaps for only a month. My dear, if I can't do this, after last night, *I'm* ruined," exclaimed Mrs. Bettersley.

The passion of vanity has its own depths in the spirit, and is powerfully militant. Mrs. Bettersley, determined to vindicate herself, disappeared for some weeks with the haunted girl. Lancelot meanwhile kept Simon company. From the ordeal their friend emerged about Christmas, possibly a little harder and brighter. If she had fought, there was not a hair displaced. She did not mention, even to Lancelot, by what arts, night and day, by what cynical vigilance she had succeeded in exorcizing the apple tree. The victory aged her, but left her as disengaged as usual. Mrs. Wing was returned to her husband. As one would expect, less and less was seen of the couple. They disappeared into happiness: a sublime nonentity.